GRADUATED AND CLUELESS

CALEB BALE

ISBN-10: 1717134386
ISBN-13: 978-1717134387

Copyright © 2018 Caleb Bale

Cover design by Lydia Emrich

All Rights Reserved. The editorial arrangement, analysis, and professional commentary are subject to this copyright notice. No portion of this book may be copied, retransmitted, reposted, duplicated, or otherwise used without the express written approval of the Author, except by reviewers who may quote brief excerpts in connection with a review.

United States laws and regulations are public domain and not subject to copyright. Any unauthorized copying, reproduction, translation, or distribution of any part of this material without permission by the Author is prohibited and against the law.

Disclaimer and Terms of Use: No information contained in this book should be considered as financial, tax, or legal advice. Your reliance upon information and content obtained by you at or through this publication is solely at your own risk. The Author assumes no liability or responsibility for damage or injury to you, other persons, or property arising from any use of any product, information, idea, or instruction contained in the content or services provided to you through this book. Reliance upon information contained in this material is solely at the reader's own risk. The Author has no financial interest in and receives no compensation from manufacturers of products or websites mentioned in this book.

Other Books by Caleb Bale

Oh, right. There aren't any.

Dedications

To my lovely wife, Bailey, who is willing to not only entertain all of my crazy ideas, but also to encourage me in them. This book is a result of that encouragement.

To my sister, Atalie, and my brother, Josiah, with whom I met every other week during the writing of this book to keep each other accountable in our goals. You guys keep me pushing myself.

To my wonderful parents, Rick and Patricia, who taught me to work hard, love well, and serve people. You are my inspiration for how I want to treat others.

To all those confused about what to do and where to go in life, especially directly after college—this is for YOU.

Acknowledgements

This book was due to a lot of encouragement from many people. But those directly involved in helping hone the book are outlined here. Thank you to Atalie Bale, my wonderful sister, who helped me edit the final book as close to perfection as possible. Thank you to Grace Vest, my good friend, who as an English fanatic was a vital editor and modifier of my sometimes unclear ways of describing things. Plus she answered question after question via text message as I was proofreading one last time. Thank you to Lydia Emrich who designed the cover of this book and helped me clarify the description on the back cover. And thank you to my family for giving insight into the content of this book. This would be a confusing, partially-complete puzzle if it weren't for everyone who helped me finish!

Contents

INTRODUCTION	**11**
LET'S GRADUATE	**13**
What People Want to Know	14
WHAT'S MOST IMPORTANT	**15**
Where The Heck Should I Live?	16
What and Where Should I Eat?	22
WHAT TO DO WITH TIME	**27**
Invest in Deep Friendships	28
Learn Voraciously	30
Build a Business	32
Be Physically Active	35
Develop Positive Habits	37
Get Involved in a Church	39
LET'S TALK JOBS AND PASSION	**43**
I Need a Job	44

Be a Linchpin	49
INSURANCE IS SO CONFUSING	**53**
The Big Auto Insurance Question	54
Do I Need Health Insurance?	56
How About Dental Insurance?	58
Life Insurance Talk	59
Psh, Disability Insurance	62
Renter's Insurance	63
Homeowner's Insurance	64
Identity Theft Protection	66
A Word About Deductibles	68
FINANCING MY LIFE	**71**
Budget (Did You Fall Asleep Yet?)	72
You Need an Emergency Fund	76
Loans	77
Now You've Got Bills!	80
Taxes, Bleh!	81
Should I Give My Hard-Earned Money Away?	85

GOOD, OLD RETIREMENT	**89**
What is a 401(k)?	91
IRA (More Letter Combinations)	93
Stocks	94
Mutual Funds	95
Bonds	96
How Much Should I Invest?	97
DATING FOR THE MASSES	**99**
Not Dating Yet? Here's How We Started	100
Points to Work Through Together	102
ADD MARRIAGE ON TOP OF ALL THIS	**107**
Preparing for Marriage	108
Preparing for the Big Day	110
Things to Change After Marriage	113
What Does My Time Look Like After the Wedding?	115
What Do Our Roles Look Like?	117
How Do Friendships Work Now?	118
How Does Family Time Look Now?	120

How Do We Handle Holidays Now?	121
Find the Time to Talk Deeply	122
NEVER STOP DREAMING	**123**
What's Next?	124
Thank You For Reading Graduated and Clueless!	**128**
Communicate with Me!	**129**
Chapter Notes	**130**

INTRODUCTION

In today's world, people my age celebrate when they do something grownup by saying they're "adulting." Using this term is partially a joke but partially not. The truth is, graduates around the world are clueless about where they want to go next in their lives. How can they pursue their dreams if they don't know how to make a budget?

In this book, I'm going to help you gain a basic understanding of topics around entering the "real world." This book is for people confused by financial terms or are simply overwhelmed by where they should live. It's for those who want to understand different types of insurance or even those who want to get married someday.

As a graduate myself, I understand the pain. I wanted a resource that would help me gain a basic understanding of what I needed to know as an adult. I wanted something that could point me to other resources to help me learn about insurance, finances, retirement, marriage, time management, etc. That's exactly why I wrote this book.

I promise that if you read this, you will experience a greater understanding of topics integral to your transition from high school or college. It will reveal subjects and issues you likely haven't considered. You'll find the examples I use easy to understand and will likely find topics to be not *quite* as intimidating as you thought.

Don't be an overwhelmed and confused graduate any longer. Be the person who is informed. Be the person who other people go to when they have questions about retirement or how to make a budget. Be the person who is proud of how they spend their time.

The tips and tricks you're about to read will help you move forward in life confidently and optimistically. Each chapter will give you new insight into life beyond the diploma. All you have to do is keep reading.

Also, side note, I hate long book introductions. So there you go. On to Part 1/Chapter 1.

PART I

LET'S GRADUATE

....

This book is not about school, though some of it may apply to you while you're in school. In my case, I did not move out until I graduated. Because I was living with my parents, I did not need to know a lot of this. I was effectively focusing solely on surviving college and obtaining the infamous piece of paper saying that I'm smart enough to help a company make a yearly profit. You may be in an entirely different situation. You may be in school and moved out. You may be planning to skip higher education altogether. Shoot, you may be an advanced 15-year-old looking to start contributing to an IRA.

Regardless, if you are in college, focus on your studies and graduate if you believe that is what you're called to do. This book isn't about how to choose a major. That's an entirely different animal that we aren't going to hunt. Having said that, let's move on to the specifics of transitioning from college or high school to the world of adults. Because you are an adult.

1

WHAT PEOPLE WANT TO KNOW

I conducted some research to find what people found helpful in their transition to the "real world" after college.

Pause One thing:

1. Ugh, the word "research" is not my favorite. It sounds like lots of numbers, graphs, and boredom. And you are very right for thinking so (if that's what you thought). However, the boredom part isn't actually true. Bear with me! Sure, I'm an engineer and I like numbers and quantifiable things, but I honestly think seeing where people fall on a spectrum (especially with colored graphs) is fascinating. You can see in picture form what people think! Ok, I'll quit geeking out.

Unpause

Here are some things to keep in mind as you read this book. I surveyed 52 people (not a huge survey but enough to get a feeling for where people landed in preparedness). I found that a huge majority of those surveyed were young people that are in the midst of transitioning. What I found most interesting was the areas of life that individuals found most helpful to their transition. Their questions frequently were related to finances (including retirement), insurance, and housing. Overall, these were very beneficial in determining specifics to discuss in this book. Thus, in the following chapters, we'll tackle these areas one by one.

Look at that, chapter 1 is done. This book will be a breeze.

PART II

WHAT'S MOST IMPORTANT

Let's assume you're graduated and prepared to move on with life. Congrats! Now, with all the change that's coming, it is very easy to be overwhelmed by the things that you need to do and learn to become a functioning adult. What is actually most important?

Good question. Let's have a one-sided discussion about this (since there aren't any ways for you to actually contribute). Let the survey and research serve as your questions and concerns!

There are three things that you are likely trying to solve at the moment:

1. Where to live
2. How/What to eat
3. Where to work (We'll look at this in a later part of the book)

Number 2 is probably a question that doesn't come to mind immediately, but it is still a basic. In the coming chapters, we'll jump into each of these.

2

WHERE THE HECK SHOULD I LIVE?

There are three possibilities you have for living arrangements.

1. Move in with the parents!
2. Rent your own place
3. Get your own house/cardboard box

<u>MOVING IN WITH THE PARENTS!</u>
Moving in with your parents is one of the most attractive options these days. Sure, you may not get along with your parents, but hey, free rent! I know many people who have chosen this option. One was living with her parents in order to start a business and grow it with less risk. One of my friends from college didn't want to stay in his small town long term, but saw living with his parents for a time as an effective way of paying off student loans as quickly as possible. Yet another friend chose to live with his parents in order to stockpile cash for his own house.

Any of those are legitimate options. However, here is my number one piece of advice when it comes to choosing to live with your parents after college: *Have an exit plan.*

Parents are a great blessing. If you are fortunate, they are encouraging and seek to help you in whatever way possible to get your feet under you. However, as financial expert Dave Ramsey says, parents are to be a safety net, not a hammock. When I suggest having an exit plan, I mean it in the best way possible. It's crucial to continue to grow and learn after college. And one of the best ways for you to do that is by living on your own. There is so much more you have to do by yourself that you don't get to do when you live with parents. Like paying for utilities, for instance, or taking your car to get regular maintenance done.

What's Most Important

If you are going to live with your parents, have a plan for when you are going to move out. Are you planning to pay off student loans? Set up a date to be all paid off, then work your butt off to get there. Are you saving up for a house? Similarly, set a date to have your down payment saved up, and start looking for houses now. It'll push you to get your housing situation down if you and your parents agree on a time for you to be moved out.

From experience, I can say that there is a big difference in others' opinions of you and your opinion of yourself when you are living on your own. You see yourself with much greater respect when you have those areas of responsibility. Living with your parents can be a great blessing when there is a plan to get out on your own! Having said that, let's move onto rent.

RENT YOUR OWN PLACE

This is the route I took after college. I was graduated for about a month and a half before my wife, Bailey, and I got married and moved into an apartment. I liked this option for us because it gave us some flexibility not only with location, but also with finances and the future in general. In the greater Columbus, Ohio area, there are a good number of rental options, whether houses or apartments. That gave us some flexibility with our location—we needed a centralized location that would work well for splitting the drive between my work and her school.

One of the best parts about renting is that all you have to do each month is pay your rent and your utilities. If the furnace goes out, you may be freezing, but at least you can chatter your teeth knowing you aren't responsible for having to replace it! In addition, renting doesn't tie you down to a specific location before you really know where you want to settle down. Bailey and I wanted to be close to school and work, but that specific location wasn't the area we wanted to be in long term.

Now, back to you. You may live in an area that doesn't have much in the way of options, but there are usually some possibilities. Look up rentals on Google and compare prices. Make sure you know what the average price is for similar rentals in your area. Is one place significantly cheaper than another? Ask questions and figure out why. Ensure you know all the specifics about renting in a specific place.

Graduated and Clueless

What are the amenities? What are their rental and late fee policies? (Side note: never be late in paying your rent.) What if you want a lease that's less than a year long? There are excellent sets of questions you can find online to aid you in locating an apartment that works for your situation. Apartments.com is an excellent source for finding the information you need before renting.[2]

Something else to consider is the security deposit that is required from you when getting a rental. The security deposit is essentially a deposit of money (in our area, normally between $200 and $750) that is usually based on your credit score. Don't have a credit score? Many places will take individuals without one but will generally require up to a full month's rent payment as the security deposit. The security deposit is accepted at the time the lease is signed and surrendered to the renter at the end of the renting season based on the condition of the apartment. So ensure you take great care of your apartment! Now for houses!

GET YOUR OWN HOUSE/CARDBOARD BOX

Houses are somewhat trickier. This is something I haven't experienced fully, but it is something that I am currently experiencing with Bailey. First of all, when looking for a house, you need to ensure you keep several things in mind:

1) Financial Situation
2) Home Location
3) Housing Market

Your financial situation is just about the most crucial part of the housing decision there is. I am a big fan of owning a house. I haven't yet, but financially, it makes sense. However, the timing is also a crucial part in your decision for a house.

Right after we got married, Bailey and I were not interested in owning a house. Sure, having a house would be nice, but it just wasn't a practical decision at the time. I had just gotten out of college and didn't have the funds necessary for a down payment. And the fact that our only expenses would be rent and utilities was a big deal when it came to convenience. But getting back to finances.

What's Most Important

When you look for a house, you need to get a realtor. The benefits of having a realtor are that they will help you find a house that meets your personal (and financial) qualifications, they'll aid in making offers on houses you like, and (possibly the biggest benefit) they can help you understand the market at the time that you are looking to buy.

Financially speaking, you are also going to want 20% or more (if possible) of the home's price for a down payment. But you aren't actually required to put a 20% down payment on your home. Loans can go all the way down to a 3% down payment. However, you should consider how that's going to affect the monthly payment. Interest is compounded; thus, if you put a 3% down payment on a home, interest will be accruing on every dollar of the principal amount. Not only will you be paying more for your principal over the same period of your loan, you will also pay interest on that extra amount as well. So if you put 3% down instead of 20%, you'll pay interest on the extra 17% that you didn't put in the down payment.

Additionally, if you put down less than a 20% down payment, PMI (Private Mortgage Insurance) will be included as an extra charge in your monthly payment. PMI essentially protects the mortgage company from your financial mistakes if you face a foreclosure. PMI can be up to 1% annually of the total value of the home. So for a $100,000 home, you could pay up to $1000 annually in PMI to the mortgage company. This isn't a dealbreaker if you're willing and able to pay it but if you can avoid it, that's ideal. The PMI will stop once the principal has been paid down to 80% of the original value. If you put down 5% ($5000) on a $100,000 home, you would pay PMI until your equity (ownership) in the house summed $20,000. Don't forget closing costs, though! These can vary from 2% to 7% of the value of the home and cover anything from appraisal to recording fees.[3] This is what the mortgage company charges to complete the mortgage process and finish the transaction with the sellers.

Next, you need your income to take care of the monthly mortgage payment. This will differ based on the mortgage you acquire. There are two conventional mortgage options (though others are available): a 30-year mortgage and a 15-year mortgage. Within these options there are also two interest options: fixed rate and variable rate.

Graduated and Clueless

As you can guess, variable rate can change and fixed rate is… well, fixed. A variable rate won't stay constant, so when the Federal Reserve lowers interest rates, your rate goes down. Nice! However, if the interest rates go up, your rate also goes up. On the contrary, a fixed rate will stay constant over the life of the mortgage. So when the rates go up or down, yours won't move. You can refinance your interest rate but that will cost you money, so it must be determined if the amount you would save on your mortgage will actually be worth the refinance fee.

One of the biggest things to consider is the length of the mortgage. With a 30-year mortgage, sure, it is longer and your monthly payment will be lower, but your interest rate is also normally higher. On the other hand, with the 15-year mortgage, it's a larger monthly payment but it will be a much greater savings over the length of the mortgage. Look at this example of purchasing a $200,000 home with a 10% downpayment of $20,000 (so a $180,000 loan). This doesn't include taxes or insurance that would be charged on top of the house payment.

15-year mortgage
Interest Rate: 4%
Monthly Payment: $1331
Total mortgage over 15 years: $239,658

30-year mortgage
Interest Rate: 4.6%
Monthly Payment: $922
Total mortgage over 30 years: $332,193

In the above example, this house is the same $200,000 home, but look at the difference in payments. Over the life of the mortgage, though the 30-year rate is only 0.6% more than the 15-year rate, the mortgage is almost $100,000 more in interest. That is more than significant. Over that 30-year mortgage, you are paying 66% more than that of the home's worth at the time of purchase.

"Ok, that's cool. I'll just get the 30-year mortgage and pay it off in 15 years. That way, if I really get into a tight spot, I can pay the minimum monthly payment."

What's Most Important

You may be saying that in your head, but consider this: even if you paid the 30-year mortgage in 15 years, you would still pay close to an extra $10,000 in interest because of the higher interest rate. Do yourself a favor and just get a smaller house that allows you to pay the 15-year monthly payment.

RESOURCES

Here is a great resource for more information on buying a home:
www.daveramsey.com/blog/how-to-buy-a-house

Apartments.com questions to ask before leasing an apartment:
www.apartments.com/blog/12-questions-to-ask-a-property-manager-before-signing-a-lease

This article from Realtor.com is great for understanding fees involved in purchasing a home: www.realtor.com/advice/finance/realtor-fees-closing-costs

3

WHAT AND WHERE SHOULD I EAT?

I'm a big fan of food (big fan). There are basically three ways to take care of your food needs and I'll outline them here.

1. Purchase groceries
2. Eat out
3. Become friends with enough people that your probability of being invited over for dinner increases significantly*

For purposes of discussion, we'll assume that from the previous chapter, you chose to move far enough away from your parents that you cannot just go to their house every night for dinner. Or breakfast and lunch, for that matter.

3. BECOME FRIENDS WITH PEOPLE
You know what, we'll tackle the third one first. Personally, I love this option. It boosts your network of friends and takes care of the necessity to eat and keeps you kicking from day to day. However, I personally don't think it is the most practical choice.

You see, friendship is a give n' take. You won't stay friends with someone if they are a take-take-take individual and, consequently, others won't be friends with you if you don't contribute in the relationship, as well. So basically, you can realistically become friends with enough people that you can exploit those friendships for food, but trust me, it'll come back to bite you (yeah, pun intended). No worries, I don't actually speak from experience in this case. But the fact of the matter is that, in America, if someone invites you over for a meal, you will generally invite them over later. Then you have to take care of the food for them. So you kind of even out. I like the option, but the practicality of executing this plan is severely lacking.

What's Most Important

1. PURCHASE GROCERIES

It's most likely that this is the way you'll have to eat to keep your budget in line (Don't have a budget? You will after I convince you in Chapter 21). At the beginning of our marriage, I actually liked grocery shopping with Bailey. I still like doing it with Bailey, but I really am not a fan of the actual shopping anymore. It takes a lot of time. Regardless, here are my pointers for grocery shopping.

Choose a good store

The area of the country in which you reside will vary in the grocery stores available to you. In Ohio, the grocery stores that are all fairly comparable in value and price are Wal-Mart, Meijer, Giant Eagle, and Kroger. Those are fine, but if you're looking to save some cash, go to a store like Aldi where the food is more discounted and still fairly high in value. If you know someone who has a Costco membership, ask if you can tag along on grocery trips where you can get items cheaper in bulk. Many people are adamant about choosing stores that hold only organic items like Whole Foods. People also get very opinionated about which companies treat their employees correctly. We're not getting into that in this book. I don't care where you shop, but choose a place that gives you what you need and fits in your budget.

You don't have to buy name-brand

Regardless of where you shop for your groceries, know that you don't have to have name-brand items. That can save you some serious cash in the long run and will help you hit your budget for the month. I am far from calling myself a food connoisseur, but a lot of the time, the generic brand tastes identical to the name brand and can save you up to 50% of the cost (sometimes more). At the end of this chapter, there is an excellent example from a blog post on the subject showing the difference between generic and name-brand items at Kroger.[1]

You may look at this and assume that generic-brand items are always cheaper. Surprisingly, they aren't! I was shocked a couple of weeks ago when I bought a block of cheese at Meijer and the name-brand block was more than a dollar less than the generic-brand block for the same amount of cheese. Also, it might be less for a name-brand item if you use a coupon. Not always, but there's a chance.

Graduated and Clueless

<u>Keep track of value for price</u>
When you're shopping, you can just grab the items you need and spend as little time in the store as possible. That's what I am always tempted to do! However, another money saving tip is maximizing value for the price. What is the weight of the cheese for what you're paying? Here's a trick for you math nerds and non-math nerds alike. On the price tag, stores always put their price per unit or weight. It'll look something like this.

**Unit Price
20¢ per oz.**

That'll help you in maximizing the value, especially when certain items are different weights. If you're going to use more shredded cheese than 8 ounces, you might as well get the 16-ounce-or-more package if price per ounce is lower. Now, be reasonable about using this strategy. Don't purchase 5 pounds of cheese just because it's going to be cheaper over the next 3 months. Where are you going to store it all? Plus, cheese gets moldy over time. I accidentally put moldy cheese in my sandwich the other day as a matter of fact. You'll need to eat that 5 pounds of cheese pretty fast.

<u>2. EAT OUT</u>
Eating out is an unbelievable temptation for me on a regular basis. Eating out just gives so many more interesting options than if I pack my lunch. Well, not always because Bailey does make some great food that she graciously allows me to pack for work, but there's a lot of restaurant food more interesting than my sandwich.

Here's another plug for a budget (remember, hit Chapter 21). It'll keep you in line with your eating out. Bailey and I have a whopping $30 in our monthly budget for eating out. So we have to use it strategically, to say the least. Regardless, if you have a maximum amount to use on eating out per month (and if you're self-controlled), it'll help curb the desire you will inevitably have if your money is going to things like paying off debt or saving for a house.

I am a fan of eating out, so I am not going to tell you that you can't do it. I just want you to control it. Not only for your financial health but

What's Most Important

also for your physical health. I mean, I can almost count on one hand the number of times that I order a salad over a burger when we go out to eat. If you control it and create a habit of making your food at home, it'll make eating out that much more enjoyable when you do it.

RESOURCES

Generic-brand vs. name-brand items: www.daveramsey.com/blog/buying-generic-groceries-saves-money

PART III

WHAT TO DO WITH TIME

Time is a new thing to adjust to when you graduate. You may have gotten a degree that didn't provide much stress and didn't require much time, leaving you with a bunch of extra time for work or other activities during school. Or you may have been like me and didn't work much in order to get all your homework and labs complete! I was in engineering and struggled to find the time for everything. There are many people who are smarter than me and worked during school, but my time was split between only a few things: school, church, and family. Other than those things, I didn't have much extra time.

When you graduate, however, you will find that if you don't have a plan for your time (just like with your money), it'll be absorbed into mindless and often frivolous things. Do you want to make a difference in the world? Make a plan for your time.

They say, "Time is money." Recently, however, I have modified that saying to "Time is more than money." Yes, you need a job, and that requires time. But if you trade all your time for money, what are you getting out of it? Is your time going to what you value most? Your financial situation will certainly determine part of your time. But for me, if I can reasonably cover something financially that will take someone else much less time to complete (e.g. working on my car), I can put my time in places that I value more.

In the coming chapters, I have outlined many suggestions for intentional and meaningful ways for you to spend your time now that college and other education is over. I want you to feel as good about the way you spend your time as you possibly can!

4

INVEST IN DEEP FRIENDSHIPS

I didn't want this chapter to be titled "Spend Time with Friends" because that title doesn't encompass the level of intensity that should be involved in real friendships. The truth is, when you're in the stage of life after college, your level of involvement with your friends has to change. When I was in college, I saw my friends daily. I talked to them daily. I suffered the woes of engineering with them daily. Post-college, however, you must intentionally seek the friends you have.

It's kind of tricky, though. You consider some people as friends in college. If you see them every day, there's a high likelihood that you talked to them daily, too. But when that daily face-to-face interaction ends, how does your friendship react? How often do you talk? Do you only send a picture in Snapchat every day to keep up your snap streak?

This may sound a bit insensitive, but you have to decide who you're going to let impact your life now. That includes the friends with whom you spend your time. You have to decide what relationships are actually worth you putting your time and energy into. Because, trust me, friendships (especially deep ones) require a lot of time and energy.

Jim Rohn, a well-known entrepreneur and motivational speaker, once said, "You are the average of the five people you spend the most time with." That quote puts things into perspective for me. How about you? Let's pretend right now that the quote only refers to the friends you have around you, not mentors, co-workers, or family. Which of your friends encourages you and helps you grow? What friends have negative attitudes?

You need friends in your life to help you grow. And by "friends," I mean close friends. Good friends. The friends that you know you can rely on and with whom you have deep relationships. If you're a guy,

What to Do with Time

you need deep friendships with men. If you're a girl, you need the same with women.

Here's another example from my life. I have several deep relationships with guys I know (again, not counting family). One lives in Mexico and challenges me constantly, not only in humility but also spiritually. I work with one friend (we were friends before working together) and he pushes me to strive for more than just "good enough." He helps me keep my thinking in a growth mentality and I can count on him to let me know what he really thinks about things. Another friend lives about forty minutes away and is a rock with whom I can discuss literally anything without feeling judged and against whom I can bounce off ideas. Another friend I meet with every week for breakfast is an encourager who helps me dream and who isn't afraid to give me his real opinion. These guys are tough guys.

Find the deep friendships. I'm sure you have friendships right now; however, they may not be deep. But it's never too late to change that. It can be awkward, but when you push your friendships deeper, asking questions and challenging opinions and habits, you will find that they'll pay off. One of my good friends and I are in similar life stages (we're both married, getting houses, etc.) and we constantly have deep discussions. We talk about what we're learning at church, in our marriages, and in life in general and I firmly believe that challenges us both. Some friends may be only interested in surface-level relationships. That's fine, but put a limited amount of your energy into these friends.

Consider who you want to be five to ten years from now and which relationships are going to affect that path positively or negatively. When you gather friends to your side with whom you can grow and learn and talk about anything, it'll greatly impact your direction. Iron sharpens iron as Proverbs 27:17 says.

In my case, the guys I mentioned are made of iron. But I have to consistently work on myself so that I'm made of iron as well. Then we can sharpen each other.

5

LEARN VORACIOUSLY

My time was absorbed in homework and projects when I was in school. But after I graduated, I had a boost in the amount of my free time, even though I took on a new job. If this is you, now what do you do?

Learn voraciously.

I have never been a big reader. Aside from school, I have read very few books in my life up to my graduation from college. Like, I'm talking less than 10. I've made excuses for myself. "I don't have enough time to read." Or "I would read but I'm way too slow for it." Or "I've been working on homework and I need to have some people time!" Truly, the only legitimate excuse of those is the last one. But the point is, I've never read much.

Since then, I heard time after time the statistics about the habits of successful people; the fact is, they read a lot of non-fiction. President Harry Truman once said, "Not all readers are leaders, but all leaders are readers." Oh, man, I want to be a leader! So I made a decision that day. I was going to read more if it killed me.

Come August of 2017, I started reading in areas that interested me, specifically in leadership, business and personal growth. I began reading a book called *The Servant* by James Hunter. It was about the character qualities of a leader. Then I read *Start With Why* by Simon Sinek about the thought process behind business strategy. Both books intrigued me with the principles they taught so I kept going. Next I read *Entreleadership* by Dave Ramsey about the workings of his business. After that I read *Good to Great* by Jim Collins about how good companies transitioned to great companies over a period of time.

What to Do with Time

The beautiful thing was that reading became more exciting and much easier. I actually got to learn about things I wanted to learn about. When I was in college, even if I liked the topic about which I was learning, homework and tests greatly decreased the joy of learning. In my experience, because I *had* to take specific classes and tests, I didn't really enjoy college that much.

You may think that business learning is boring and not your thing. That's okay! But start reading about things that *do* interest you. Like really interest you. Get excited about reading and learning again. Graduation wasn't the end of learning; graduation was the beginning of a whole new kind of learning for me! In the last six months, I've read twelve books and am working on my thirteenth. I have a goal of reading twenty-two books this year and I'm not planning on stopping when I hit it.

But reading isn't the only thing that you can do to learn. Want to learn to code a website or an app? There are tons of free resources about that online. You can even take online courses for free. Want to learn how to use your camera more effectively? Do it because you'll see photography in a whole new light.

The key is, start learning more. Push yourself to learn what you want. It'll open up your perspective on life and learning in general.

6

BUILD A BUSINESS

This is a topic about which I am particularly passionate. There is an incredible number of people who hate their jobs. In fact, a recent Gallup poll found that 85% of employees worldwide hate their jobs.[1] I believe that you don't have to hate your job, and starting a business could be your answer over the long term. Now, starting a business will likely start out as a side hustle. You probably won't have the funding to start a business and work for it full-time. But you can start one and it can grow.

Starting a business is actually quite simple. As Christy Wright, a small-business expert and founder of Business Boutique, says, "All you need is a name and a Facebook page." As business increases, you will need to register it with the state and the IRS, but you don't need to jump through all the hoops to have an officially registered name with the state in order to conduct business. You'll just need to report your earnings as income on your taxes.

The key is to find something that you love to do and figure out how you can use it to solve problems for people. Businesses will fall into one of two categories: a product or a service. In the product category, you may be able to sell photos you take, pictures you paint, or, in the case of one guy I know, wooden sculptures carved by a chainsaw. Can you crochet or knit? Find people for whom you can make custom scarves.

"But I don't have the skills to make anything!" This is where the second type of business comes in: services. What do you love to do that will allow you to serve people? In my case, I love filmmaking. I love developing a creative video that I can deliver to a customer. Consider weddings. There is almost no better feeling that I get than when I get to show a newly married couple the edited music video of their special day.

What to Do with Time

What do you love? Are you tech-savvy? There are plenty of elderly people who try to set up e-readers and iPads but don't know how to use them. That right there is a problem you can solve. Start a business that helps teach them. Do you like to spend time outdoors getting your hands dirty? You can change that into a landscaping business in your area. There are people everywhere that hate to move leaves or mow their lawns. There is almost no limit to business possibilities!

I'm kind of a business junkie. I don't know why, but I find it fascinating and have been learning a lot more about it recently. Donald Miller, a *New York Times* Bestselling Author, wrote one book that I read in the past several months called *Building a Storybrand*. This is one of the best books I've read in the past year because it gives an enormous amount of practical knowledge and advice. The premise of the book is that you need to brand yourself as the guide in your customer's story. Your customer feels they need to be the hero in their story, and when you can make that emotion come to life, they will see you as a character that can fit into their story.

Thus, you need to be painfully clear about how you are going to help your customer. This is an aspect of my business that I've spent a great deal of time on. For example, after I read the book, I noticed how much more clarity my website needed in order to convey my message about my filmmaking business. I needed to make clear my desire to help the customer become the hero in their story. Likewise, if you want to develop a business, you need to be painfully clear about how you will help your customer. If you start a landscaping business, help your customer understand that they will love their lawn and it will stand out above other lawns in the neighborhood (who doesn't want that?). If you help your customer solve a problem and feel like a hero, you've got a good chance at building a successful business.

Graduated and Clueless

RESOURCES

Gallup Poll: <u>news.gallup.com/opinion/chairman/212045/world-broken-workplace.aspx?</u>
<u>g_source=position1&g_medium=related&g_campaign=tiles</u>

These are some of the best resources I have for you for building a business. All three books have excellent podcasts as well:

1. *Building a Storybrand* by Donald Miller
2. *Entreleadership* by Dave Ramsey
3. *Business Boutique* by Christy Wright

7

BE PHYSICALLY ACTIVE

Physical activity - Bleh. That's how I looked at it many times in college. I love being active and fit, but it was tough in school. I found that in my freshman and sophomore years, my tri-weekly runs with my cousin did a wonder for my stress levels. The act of getting outside and pounding the asphalt made me an overall happier student to be around. As I hit my junior, senior, and super senior years (fifth year of college for those who couldn't finish in four), I started pushing off physical activity because I was afraid I'd fall behind in classes. Realistically, I'm sure that if I had kept it up, it would have helped me do better in college with much less worrying.

Regardless, when you graduate, you need to ensure that you set aside at least some time to remain physically active. You can be like most people and aim to become physically fit, or you can be like me—work out so you don't have to worry about the calories you take in. Kidding, I want to be at least a little fit.

At the end of 2017, Bailey and I got a flyer from a local gym that was opening up at the beginning of the year. I automatically thought, "Give me a break, do they really think I am going to fall for paying a gym to work out throughout the year?" Then I saw it.

Only $10 a month!

"Wellllll, I guess I haven't ever been much into working out, but I don't have any other plans and that's really a pretty good deal and I guess I could just try to make a new year's resolution and try to beat all the people that only make it through January and it would be pretty sweet if I got super ripped." Run-on sentences sound much better in my head. I don't like being persuaded by an advertisement, but it sounded good, so Bailey and I signed up.

Graduated and Clueless

I set some specific and measurable goals for working out and I can tell you that it is one of the most satisfying things I've gotten to do since graduating. Some people will work their legs, then the next day they work their arms, then the next day they work their core. I don't like to go that much during the week, so I just do what I can in the time that I've got. Bailey and I tend to go three times a week, which is much more than I've ever done before. Like at least 300% more than I've done and it's been satisfying. I'm no fitness guru but I am making progress.

Your thing might not be the gym. If you don't know what it is, try out several things. My cousin isn't a gym person, but he runs and bikes quite a bit (though he's probably still been to the gym more than me). According to the Mayo Clinic, physical activity will scientifically lower your stress.[1] Do yourself a favor and get moving.

Also, if anyone reading this is a fitness guru and wants to give me free tips on working out more effectively, hit me up by contacting me through the "Contact Me" section at the back of this book. I'm all about free tips.

RESOURCES

Mayo Clinic: www.mayoclinic.org/healthy-lifestyle/stress-management/in-depth/exercise-and-stress/art-20044469

8

DEVELOP POSITIVE HABITS

Habits have the potential to help you grow and they have the potential to hold you down. Poor habits can hurt you in the short term, but can really hurt in the long term. They can even end your life prematurely if you have poor health habits. But when positive habits are used to discipline yourself, the ROI (Return on Investment) will pay off beyond what you might expect.

John Maxwell, a leading voice on personal and leadership growth, puts a large amount of emphasis on consistency and habits in his book *The 15 Invaluable Laws of Growth*. He says that the Law of Consistency (another name for habits) is one of the most important laws in which to invest. He says this because consistency, when utilized in light of positive habits, will lead to a lot of other personal growth. Here's an example from my own life.

When I graduated, I wouldn't say I had very many good habits. I wouldn't necessarily say I had many bad habits either, but my good habits were severely lacking. Since then, I've been working on developing good habits in three areas of my life: spiritual habits, physical habits, and learning habits.

Spiritually, as Christians, Bailey and I set a goal of reading at least a snippet of the Bible every night. "Every night" doesn't make for a very good goal, but within the first year of marriage, I think we've missed maybe ten or eleven nights of reading a portion of the Bible together before bed. This doesn't always produce particularly productive conversation, as we are frequently tired. However, I have no doubt about its effectiveness in developing a stronger relationship between Bailey and I, as well as developing a similar outlook on life in us. This also helps us grow together in our walks of faith because we talk about each passage after we read it.

They say that it takes twenty-one days to develop a habit. Before we got married, I asked Bailey that we read the Bible together every

Graduated and Clueless

day for twenty-one days to develop this habit, and it has happened. Even when we are exhausted, one of us will say, "All right, ready to listen to me read my Bible?" It keeps us focused on God and our spiritual growth.

Physical habits have been difficult for me to develop over the years. I tend to have a high metabolism, so I haven't ever had any weight issues. However, it takes a lot for me to convince myself that going on a run will be better for me than staying in and watching another episode of whatever I'm watching on Netflix (can I hear an amen?). Accountability helps me personally, so in my first and second year of college, my cousin, Jacob, and I consistently ran three to seven miles three times a week. And my stress levels in school drastically improved.

Since the beginning of 2018, Bailey and I have been working on developing our physical habits, and it's been fairly successful. We go to the gym three times a week because of my 2018 goal of hitting it at least ten times a month. By now, we have a habit set and it has made working out regularly immensely easier. Not to mention the fact that, physically speaking, I've felt much better with consistent exercising.

Learning habits are something that I've had to pursue a bit more intentionally since graduation. I have had a lot more time than when I was in school. And since I wasn't being educated in an institution anymore, I had to change things up. So I made reading goals. In 2018 alone, I have a goal to read 4500 pages of books. That breaks down to 12.3 pages a day. I have developed a habit of reading every day over my lunch break and when I get home. It has pushed me to consistently learn and grow. Side note, as of writing this section, I am two weeks ahead of schedule in my reading goal.

In my opinion, habits have a much greater power over you when you develop them intentionally. It creates a discipline that will treat you well in the future. An individual who has discipline has a leg up in life. They can force themselves more easily to do things that aren't pleasant but will have a high return on investment. Many times, even in areas in which an individual doesn't currently have any habits, that learned discipline will benefit them.

9

GET INVOLVED IN A CHURCH

This book isn't geared only toward Christians. However, I am a Christian, so I wanted to cover some of the topics in the more spiritual nature because these were things I struggled with as I neared graduation—things like church choice, quiet time, and others. You may not be a Christian or consider yourself spiritual at all. You don't even have to read this section if you don't want to. I'm not going to make you (plus I can't since you're on the other side of this book). But if you do, I hope that it encourages you if you are struggling with similar things.

So, why are there so many churches? And where should you go? In response to the first question, it is because people have many differing opinions. It's as simple as that. To the second question, I can't answer that. There are so many variations of worship. One may be better for you over another. Some churches have a contemporary type of worship while others have a traditional (liturgical) style. But which one is the right one?

Bailey and I attend a Lutheran Church Missouri Synod (LCMS). We grew up in the Lutheran church, which has a lot to do with where we attend, but we think this is the place where we can serve God the best at the moment. It really can get very confusing when people talk about denominations or even when they talk about non-denominational churches. What the heck is the difference between Catholics, Lutherans, Methodists, Presbyterians, Pentecostals, and Baptists? We're not going to get into that. That is, needless to say, beyond the scope of this book. However, I will say that your salvation isn't dependent upon going to a specific denomination of a church. Thank goodness! I believe that when we Christians get to Heaven, it will be made up of people that belonged to a variety of denominations on Earth. It's just that all these people will have believed in the saving blood of Jesus Christ and repented of their sins.

Graduated and Clueless

Bailey and I are Lutheran because we agree with more of the Lutheran perspectives on Christianity than any other denomination (or even non-denomination). What is vitally important, however, is that whatever church you go to has the major points of Christianity correct. I firmly believe this must be true about the church you attend if you want a place that is conducive to your spiritual growth in Christ.

Your church *must* teach that we are naturally sinful and that the result of our sin is eternal damnation (Romans 6:23). Your church *must* teach that we cannot save ourselves with good works (Ephesians 2:8-9). Your church *must* teach that God's son, Jesus Christ, through His death and resurrection, is the absolute only way to obtain salvation from sin (John 3:16). Your church *must* teach that the third person of the Trinity, the Holy Spirit, is ready to work in your life if you open yourself to Him. Your church *must* teach that the Bible is the inerrant word of God and have a desire to be faithful in practice of its teachings. Your church *must* be sacramental. This means that they believe that as Christians, they will follow Christ's commands to commune in the Lord's Supper regularly and be baptized into the faith. And your church should be accountable to some larger church body. Just like a Christian trying to live life alone without other Christians around, a church without accountability in its theology can veer off the true teachings of the Bible. Though there are many other aspects to choosing a theologically sound church, these are the absolute essentials.

You need to choose a church that provides you a worshipful experience. You need to choose a church in which you can serve God with others. You need a firm, Bible-believing church that teaches what the Bible says, not what people want to hear. You need to choose a church in which you can be plugged into a personal group; this is a group in which you can be encouraged and can encourage your fellow believers. You need to choose a church that challenges you to seek God and grow in your relationship with Him everyday. Christianity isn't a Sunday thing, it's an everyday thing. Having said all this, I think there's one more very important thing to say about church-choosing.

There is no perfect church. And there won't be until the end of time when Christ comes again. Every church has its issues; trust me.

The key is choosing one that is theologically sound and teaches what the Bible says.

Just don't get stuck at a point where you don't go to church because you don't know which one is the best. It's a place where you will experience God's work, His encouragement through others, and spiritual growth. You can't get that in the way God intended if you don't go to church.

QUIET TIME

As for "quiet time," this can vary quite a bit from person to person. Quiet time is generally what Christians call their time to read and study the Bible and pray. I try to get to work early enough that I can read some of my Bible before I start working. This is nice because it's a great way to get into the right frame of mind before beginning the day. However, evening may be more of your speed. If you're not a morning person and can concentrate much better later in the day, evening would likely be a more effective time for you. Bailey and I will read some of the Bible together every evening, even if it is just a few verses. We talk about it and what we gathered from it. It's a great way to connect spiritually on a regular basis. But no one is perfect and Bailey will readily attest to the fact that when I'm tired, I will start saying things that have absolutely no connection whatsoever to what we read. Like I said, evening might be for you but it might not.

OTHER SPIRITUAL LEARNING

A couple of other things I like to do to grow in my faith is by reading spiritual growth books and listening to sermons. One book I'm currently reading is *The Christian Atheist* by Craig Groeschel about living consistently with how we believe. Earlier this year, I also read *The Treasure Principle* by Randy Alcorn about generosity and how it applies to us spiritually (this is an excellent book, by the way). One of my goals at the beginning of this year was to listen to five sermons per week apart from the ones I hear on Sundays.

I like these methods of learning because I believe that constant interaction with God's word, even if it is indirectly through another book or a sermon, reminds me every day of God's promises and His forgiveness and my need for a savior. Subconsciously, I think it strengthens my faith and prepares me for difficult and trying times.

PART IV

LET'S TALK JOBS AND PASSION

In the survey I took for this book, I found that job searching and other career information proved to be one of the most requested topics to discuss. How do you find an employer that will pay you enough for you to live? A lot of students make their way out of college with plans to do something fun that will make them a living at the same time. The dreams you have are what will get you to new, exciting areas of your life. Sometimes, you'll need to work a job that you aren't as passionate about as you make your way to your dream.

Ken Coleman, a professional at asking questions and giving advice to individuals who feel stuck in their jobs, tells a story about how it took him seven years to work his way into a full-time radio career while he worked other jobs that didn't involve his passions. Now, he helps people reach their "sweet spot." Ok, time for an official Ken-Coleman definition:

Sweet Spot: Where your top talents and your top passions intersect.

On his program, *The Ken Coleman Show*, Coleman helps people discover what their talents and passions are. Then, he helps them find a path to getting into the field in which they want to work.

One of my favorite quotes ever comes from the author and civil rights leader, Howard Thurman, who said, "Don't ask what the world needs. Ask what makes you come alive, and go do it. Because what the world needs is people who have come alive." Where's your sweet spot?

This section is about your job and how to be vital in whatever role you are in. I sincerely hope that you are already in your sweet spot but if not, I hope this prompts you onto the next steps in reaching your sweet spot.

10

I NEED A JOB

You're graduated. Yay! A lot of graduates, especially nowadays, are finding it difficult to get a job in their chosen field while making enough to pay off all their student loans. Students want the perfect situation: a high-paying job with good benefits, passionate work, an ideal location, etc. It seems to be a problem that is constantly faced in our society (I face it too). Personally, I had to do what I would call "settling" in some of these areas. I have a forty-five minute drive to work every day. That is not what I would call ideal. However, it does give me a lot of time to learn from "Automobile University," a Zig Ziglar term for listening to audiobooks in the car. I wanted to be close to family and church, as well as not too far from Columbus so that when Bailey started school on the main campus of Ohio State, it wouldn't be a nightmare drive. I already had a job after college, so we had to give something up, and that was living close to work.

If you don't already have a job lined up for when you graduate, consider these pieces of advice:

1. Seek career advice from your college or university
2. Seek jobs online
3. Ask people around you for help and suggestions

SEEK CAREER ADVICE FROM YOUR COLLEGE

Chances are, your college has tons of resources available for current students and graduating seniors for job searching—not only for a full-time position, but also for internships. But since we're talking about transitioning from college, we'll focus on the graduating seniors. At Ohio State, they have a website called "Buckeye Careers." It is where students can go to put in their information, resumes, etc., and receive information from recruiters for positions. Within the context of large

Let's Talk Jobs and Passion

universities, this is a great option because companies all over the nation are interested in students from Ohio State and similar schools.

You may not go to a large school, but that doesn't mean they don't have ways to help. A good number of schools have large career fairs where recruiters will come into the school on a specific day, allowing students to visit booths and give resumes to potential employers personally. This is another great option. I liked it because I felt like that gave me a much higher likelihood of an employer being interested in me. They could see me face to face and discuss my passions and experience in a more personal interaction. One of my friends got called by two or three different employers for official interviews after going to a job fair and was subsequently given job offers. In my experience, Ohio State had a large career fair with many different industries attending. They also had many more focused career fairs that were even better to attend. In my case, they had a career fair specifically for engineers.

SEEK JOBS ONLINE

There are almost innumerable jobs posted online every day. However, this is a trickier way of obtaining a job. I was never contacted by any company when I submitted an application online. It's not very personal, and all they are looking at are things on a piece of paper. They don't get to experience you talking about your passions or experiences you've had or things that you've learned. By all means, do the searches and apply for jobs. People get jobs with their online applications all the time. It may pay off and it gives you a better understanding of the types of jobs in which you may be interested. I just personally found it difficult to seek employment online. The key is, if you submit online applications, do a lot of them. The more you do, the more likely it is you will get a hit and some interest.

ASK PEOPLE AROUND YOU FOR HELP AND SUGGESTIONS

One of the absolute best books I've ever read is a book called *The Power of Who* by Bob Beaudine.[1] The premise of the book is this: you already know everyone you need to know. Most networking books focus on meeting new people and giving out business cards.

Graduated and Clueless

Beaudine argues, though, that this isn't an effective way of networking. Think about this.

Beaudine says that everyone you know fits into a category: your fans, acquaintances, advocates, allies, "Who" friends, and inner circle. He focuses specifically on the "Who" friends. This is how he describes them:

> One of life's pleasant little phenomena is that once someone holds a special place in your heart, they never really leave. These are friends—not acquaintances. An acquaintance who likes you will wish you well. But a friend will actually help you— starting now because they care about you. You're special to them in the same way they're special to you. They will laugh with you, cry with you, and even fight for you if need be. If you're traveling through their town, you'd rather sleep on their couch than in a king-size bed at the Hilton. Friendship has a mystical quality that you can't really explain. True friendship is based entirely on love, loyalty, and mutual regard. There are no strings attached. Your "Who" friends will help you—just because! (36)

Your "Who" friends are not part of your inner circle mostly because of time and distance constraints. But it doesn't change the fact that they would help you with anything, even if they didn't get anything out of it. Beaudine completely opened my mind with where he took the concept of "Who" friends. You have "Who" friends. We all do. Some have more than others, but everyone has them. This means that since you have "Who" friends and since your "Who" friends have "Who" friends, you're automatically connected to exponentially more people than you may have thought. Sure, traditional networking has this same relationship. However, this is where The Power of Who separates itself from traditional networking because your "Who" friends actually care about you and are willing to go to greater lengths to help you.

Now, think about the people you know. Let's look at school. If you are graduating soon (or already have), think about the professors you had. Which ones did you get along with especially well? There is a very high likelihood that they are more than happy to help you if you

Let's Talk Jobs and Passion

ask. I had several professors like this. I also got to know the department chairman who was understandably well connected in my field of study. I had developed a reputation of working hard and doing my best on homework and projects, so I brought some weight to our discussions. He was more than happy to help me find a job in my field if I didn't already have one. I know he contacted some large companies with whom he was connected for a friend of mine looking for an internship.

Now, think about people your parents know. Frequently your parents' "Who" friends are ecstatic to aid you in your search for a job or opportunity. Ask your parents if any of their friends are connected in the vocation in which you want to be. Finally, what about your other "Who" friends from church, work, or the gym? Whoever these friends are, you need to tell them what you want to do. If you don't tell them, they can't help you. If you do tell them, they will keep you in mind when opportunities arise. Plus, when you mention your interests, those friends may respond, "Hey, I know so-and-so and they do almost the exact thing you're interested in!"

The reason I wanted to talk about this type of networking is because, honestly, I don't have much experience at all with finding a job or jobs. I mean, I'm a recent college grad myself! However, this "Who"-friends thought process has impacted my thinking in a dramatic way. I actually do have experience with this. I look back on my job searching experience and I can see exactly where these principles fall into my life.

In the summer of 2015, I was transitioning into my junior year at Ohio State in agricultural engineering. I had searched the whole previous semester for engineering internship positions in companies nearby. I had gone to career fairs and submitted many online applications. No bites. I then mentioned my frustrations with trying to find an internship to a friend. In fact, it was a friend who had graduated from Ohio State with the same degree. He proceeded to say, "You know, I could probably get you an internship at the place that I work if you want." Feeling rather defeated from the lack of company interest in my resumes, I was ecstatic!

I did, indeed, get an internship that summer. In fact, my boss asked me if I'd be willing to do some part-time work for them over the school year, for which I was grateful. Again, I spent the next summer

Graduated and Clueless

and the following school year working for them doing design work. In my last semester as a student, they offered me a full-time, salary position, which I accepted. I love the people and enjoy the work. And I've gotten several other people internships and interviews as their "Who" friend.

This is a different and more effective way of looking for a job if you don't already have much experience. And, in many ways, it's a great way to search for work, even if you do have experience.

11

BE A LINCHPIN

In his book, *Linchpin*, Seth Godin outlines what it takes to become a "linchpin," someone who is indispensable.[1] This applies not only in work, but also in the rest of life. He encourages the reader to be unique by outlining some specific ways to pursue their dream and make a difference in the lives of others. I recommend the book because it has many applicable sections. One of the most impactful parts for me was where he talked about the human's "lizard brain."

The lizard brain is an unsophisticated way of describing that part of your brain that wants to be lazy. It's the part that wants to relent to the easy things. Watching TV and scrolling through social media is a small part of the lizard brain. On a larger scale, the lizard brain keeps you doing things that don't require much emotional energy.

Godin calls this "emotional labor." He says this on the topic: "The only way to get what you're worth is to stand out, to exert emotional labor, to be seen as indispensable, and to produce interactions that organizations and people care deeply about" (27). How? Emotional labor. That is why someone at a fast food restaurant is so replaceable (no offense). The job doesn't require emotional labor. You show up, you make fries, and you leave.

Godin's first suggestion involves choosing something that requires emotional labor and is not asymptotic in nature. When something is "asymptotic," it means there is a limit to how good you can get at it. He used bowling as an example. The best score you can get is 300 points. That's it. So you're closer to becoming a linchpin when you choose something at which you can always get better and in which you can grow. You become indispensable.

This is where being an artist comes in. To be a linchpin is to be an artist. He doesn't talk about artists in the sense of those who can paint, draw, and sculpt. In fact, he has a section specifically labeled "Artists Who Can't Draw." Godin's argument is that literally anyone can

Graduated and Clueless

become an artist. The reason is because the word "art" is intrinsically deeper than what is conventionally understood. Art is anything that requires emotional labor. What do you put your heart into? That is what requires emotional labor.

And it doesn't have to be "artistic" in nature. Recently, a coworker of mine told me that he isn't a creative individual because he is an engineer. Having read this book, I countered, "Don't give me that. You are an engineer, which means that you are creative. You have to develop creative ways to solve problems and make designs more efficient and effective!" Godin thinks that even in the midst of seemingly meaningless work, you can still be an artist. He says, "I think art is the ability to change people with your work, to see things as they are and then create stories, images, and interactions that change the marketplace" (91).

However, it goes deeper than that. Godin argues that being a linchpin stems from generosity: "Becoming a linchpin is not an act of selfishness. I see it as an act of generosity, because it gives you a platform for expending emotional labor and giving gifts" (153).

Essentially, you are an artist and a linchpin when you are giving what you put your heart into as a gift. That gift may come with monetary compensation, but it can still be a gift. He used the beginning of the computer operating system called "Linux" as an example. When Linus Torvalds developed the system, he gave it as a gift to his friends. But when the popularity spread, he became a linchpin because his gift turned into something that helped people domestically and internationally. When you are generous, you become a linchpin. When you go the extra mile for a customer, you are a linchpin. When you find ways to make your boss's life easier, you are a linchpin.

What this book did for me was expand my view of art and creativity. It helped me understand more about the creativity of all individuals and how it isn't confined to just those who are "right-brained." Godin gives a very detailed perspective of how artistry creates indispensability, and his book helped me understand more about how I can apply those principles to my own work.

At my job, I try to let my boss know that if there is anything that he needs done that would be a better use of my time than his, I am willing to do it. This makes me a linchpin because I am not just there to

Let's Talk Jobs and Passion

do my job; I'm willing to help him with his so that he can boost his own productivity. Find ways that you can become indispensable in your job. Your job may not require much emotional labor, but find ways that you can put your heart into it. Be willing to do the small things. Go the extra mile and do things that aren't a part of your job description. Have such unbelievably excellent customer service that your customers will never forget their experience because it was that good. That's what will keep people coming back. That's what will make your actions stand out to your boss.

PART V

INSURANCE IS SO CONFUSING

....

Needless to say, insurance is a necessary evil for all of us. It can certainly be a blessing because if you actually need it for housing, vehicular, or medical reasons, it'll help keep you from becoming financially broken. It can make the recovery from an accident or a house fire much less stressful! However, I say a necessary evil because, let's be honest, who wants to pay for something that they may not even need? Plus, it's incredibly confusing. There are seemingly a million different types of insurance. And what the heck is a deductible?

The major thing I want you to take from this introduction is that you need insurance to ensure your relative financial security and ensure you aren't a burden to family. As a young person, it's easy to realize why you will need something like car insurance (even without mentioning that it's the law). But it's easy to think that you won't get sick and won't need health insurance. Insurance is essentially a gamble and sometimes you want to gamble on your own health. But you need it nonetheless.

In this part, we'll cover a bunch of insurance types and look at why you might need or might not need a specific insurance. We'll look at health, dental, disability, car, renter's, and homeowner's insurance. In addition, we'll cover some of the terminology and help you understand some different kinds of policies.

Onward!

12

THE BIG AUTO INSURANCE QUESTION

How much auto insurance do you need? Notice: I did not ask if you *needed* auto insurance. In most states, it is required by law. However, there are many levels of auto insurance, and understanding those on a surface level will help you understand if you need to purchase coverage or if you need to re-evaluate your current policy.

There are five main sections to consider when it comes to auto insurance. The descriptions following each section assume that the accident is your fault. Hopefully, if an accident isn't your fault, the other individual is covered and their insurance should cover any expenses associated with the accident. Here are the areas of auto coverage:

1. Liability coverage
2. Comprehensive coverage
3. Collision coverage
4. Medical Expenses coverage
5. Uninsured, Underinsured coverage

Liability coverage: For an accident that is your fault, this will cover property damage or medical expenses for individuals affected.
Comprehensive coverage: This will cover any damages that occur to your car due to natural disasters, theft, or any other things that cause damage. The only exception to this coverage is collisions.[1]
Collision coverage: This will cover your vehicle repairs in the event that there is a collision that is your fault or even someone else's fault (maybe from a hit-and-run).
Medical Expenses coverage: This is what will cover medical expenses (due to a collision) for you and/or your passengers, regardless of health insurance status.
Uninsured, Underinsured coverage: If you are involved in an accident in which you are not liable but the other individual doesn't have

Insurance is so Confusing

insurance (or doesn't possess the state minimum of insurance), this is what will cover any expenses that occur.

Each of these coverages is part of a typical auto insurance policy. You can, however, choose how much of each you want in your insurance policy, assuming that you hit the state minimum. Talk to an insurance professional for advice on what coverage you need. There is also a link in the resources section of this chapter outlining generally how much coverage you need.[2]

Here's a good money-saver tip: when you are looking for insurance, go to an independent insurance broker. A broker will find what the ideal coverages are for you and shop among a lot of insurance companies to find the best coverage that will save you the most money. Don't go to one specific insurance company and ask them to give you the policy you need. They can only go so low on their own insurance. But if you use an independent agent, you'll have many more options.

RESOURCES

This is not the department of motor vehicles. However, it does provide some helpful information about coverage:
www.dmv.org/insurance/vehicle-coverages.php

How much car insurance do you need? Check this out:
www.daveramsey.com/blog/how-much-car-insurance

13

DO I NEED HEALTH INSURANCE?

Yes.

As a young person, it's easy to think that you will have good health for forever. But if something happens and you don't have insurance, you'll have to pay for all the expenses. It's important to realize that health insurance is not only going to help pay for things like surgeries that you need; it will also help pay for prescriptions if need be.

Health insurance generally comes in two ways—through an employer or through the marketplace. Insurance through your employer is often the preferred means of getting insurance because the employer will often cover a good percentage of your insurance premium. For example, my current employer covers 80% of my health insurance premium, making insurance *much* more affordable for me.

Another nice thing is that if you are married (or even have a family), you can get health insurance for your spouse and kids through your employer. If you and your spouse work, you can choose between your two employers for where you want to get insurance. One might cover 70% of your premiums while the other covers 80%, so it's obvious with whom you should get your insurance, especially if the coverage is comparable.

Within the realm of health insurance, it's likely you've heard the term "pre-existing condition." It's one of those big words that is easy to glaze over if you don't know what it is but fairly easy to understand if someone explains it to you. Essentially, it is any medical condition that you or someone else on your policy has before obtaining health insurance. However, based on current laws, no health insurance companies in the marketplace are allowed to decline an individual with a pre-existing condition. Plus, they can't charge you more because of it either. This is good if you have cancer or asthma and are in need of insurance.[1]

Insurance is so Confusing

RESOURCES
HealthCare.gov on pre-existing conditions: www.healthcare.gov/coverage/pre-existing-conditions

14

HOW ABOUT DENTAL INSURANCE?

Dental insurance, in my opinion, is the insurance that is frequently neglected because teeth are frequently neglected. Nobody likes the dentist (except my editor, Grace). Do you know how many dentist jokes there are? Okay, not many that I've heard, but when it comes to talking about the dentist's office, there seems to be a fine line between the office and a torture chamber. In spite of this, dental insurance is a must in my opinion. It is incredibly cheap and well worth the price, assuming that you value your teeth and have regular dental appointments. Do you like eating solid food? You probably want to care for your teeth. Let me give you an example from my own life.

At my work, I have $4 deducted from every paycheck for dental insurance. That's about $8 per month. I go to the dentist twice a year. Yes, twice. I am a brave man. In the last couple months, I got a normal cleaning by a hygienist and I got X-rays taken of my teeth. This and several other things they did would have cost me $277 for one visit, but my dental insurance covered $265. That left me with a bill for $12. That's it. Combined, I pay about $104 for dental insurance per year. In this one visit, I saved $161. That's a win!

One thing to note: this is the bill for a very healthy mouth. I've never had a cavity. What does that mean if you don't have healthy teeth? That's right, more expenses for fillings, crowns, etc. Dental insurance will save you a lot of money. I'd suggest getting it.

15

LIFE INSURANCE TALK

Health insurance is for your benefit to keep you alive. Life insurance, ironically, is for when you're dead. This means that if you have a life insurance policy when you die, the money from that policy will go to a beneficiary you have named to cover burial costs and any debts you may owe. In many circumstances, it's also intended to aid in living expenses. Again, it's a gamble. However, it's not necessarily a must for you. It just depends on what life stage you are currently in. We'll cover this later in the chapter. There are many kinds of life insurance policies but we'll cover the two most frequently purchased: whole life and term life insurance. I know it can feel a little morbid at times, but let's look at both in a bit more detail.

Whole life insurance is considered a method of savings by many financial institutions. They don't like the idea of you throwing your money away at something you may not need. Whole life insurance is a cash-value policy and will put part of your money towards your insurance and the other part towards a cash value portion (the savings). Essentially, if you choose to end the policy, you can get the cash value out of it. It won't be nearly what you put into it, but it will be something.

Term life insurance is exactly what it sounds like; it covers a term of your life. Generally speaking, you can get 20-year or 30-year term policies though there are other options. If you die, your beneficiary (usually your spouse or family) will get the money from the policy to cover burial costs and pay off your debts. Let's say you are a 25-year-old and you are married and have a $250,000 term life policy on yourself. You have $100,000 of private student loan debt (that's a lot of zeros). If you died, about $10,000 would go towards covering your burial (unless your family wants you to RIP in a stylish coffin) and $100,000 would go towards paying off your student loans (since

Graduated and Clueless

they're private). Your spouse would receive $140,000, which could help with paying for a house or paying down more student loans.

The big difference between whole life and term life insurance is the length of the policy and price. The whole life policy can be held for your entire life. The term insurance will last for only the term that you specify. However, term insurance will cost you about 10% of whole life, depending on where you get it. Now, that is a big difference. That's why Dave Ramsey, a financial talk-show host, avidly suggests to not go with the whole life policy.

"But doesn't the whole life policy have cash value? Isn't that an investment?" Yes, it does. But it's not really an investment because overall, you don't get nearly the other 90% of the money you put into whole life compared to term life. Chris Hogan, in his book *Retire Inspired,* says this about whole life policies: "I recommend only term life insurance; whole life or cash value plans are bad ideas. They may look good at first because they have a savings plan built in, but I always want you to keep your insurance and your investing separate. You'll make the best use of your money by paying for term life (more coverage for less money) and investing in the retirement plans we've already discussed" (203).

The key to life insurance is that you must have it if there are people that are depending on you financially. Are you married? Do you have a mortgage and kids? You probably need a hefty policy. That way, they can pay off all your loans, and have some on which to live. In my case, I am married, but have no debt and no kids. My company automatically carries 1.5 times the salary of each employee in term life insurance. I, however, got another policy so that in the improbable event of my parachute not opening while skydiving, Bailey would be able to pay for my burial and the rest of her education and living expenses without even having to worry about working during that time.

Dave Ramsey suggests that people have 10-12 times their annual income in a term life insurance. Here's another example. If you make $50,000 a year and are debt free with a family, you would purchase approximately $500,000 of term life insurance. If an accident occurred and (God forbid) you died, Ramsey suggests that the insurance money would be invested into good growth-stock mutual funds. Assuming the investment brought 10% interest annually, that would keep your

Insurance is so Confusing

family living without the need of a job for years to come. Your spouse could get $50,000 per year from the investment, allowing them to keep the same standard of living without changing the amount they work. Plus, the money could aid in paying for college once your kids were grown enough to attend.

Remember, life insurance is for people who are depended upon for their economic value. If you are the sole breadwinner in the family, your spouse and your kids depend on you to live. If your wife is a stay-at-home mom, she is still providing economic value because she is taking care of the kids. In the unfortunate event of her death, you would likely have to pay for childcare some other way. That's economic value, even though she doesn't work outside of the house.

One last thing: you do not need life insurance if you have an emergency fund and you don't have anyone depending on you. Are you a new college graduate and unmarried with an emergency fund? Chances are, you don't need life insurance. Just make sure that your emergency fund can cover your burial since all other debts would be cancelled in the event of your death.

RESOURCES

Here's a great resource for understanding more about life insurance: www.daveramsey.com/blog/term-life-vs-whole-life-insurance

16

PSH, DISABILITY INSURANCE

What is disability insurance, anyways? I mean, I don't personally hear about it much. It is, nonetheless, very important. If you get into an accident at work or away from work that leaves you disabled in the short term, or even permanently, how are you going to pay your bills? What if you literally can't do any work from your 30s on?

Disability insurance will avert this risk. There are a couple types of disability insurances: short-term and long-term. Short-term probably isn't necessary if you have a large emergency fund (say, 3-6 months). Long-term insurance, however, will provide you with consistent income, allowing you to eat and go to the movies while you can't work (what else are you gonna do with your time? Knit?).

Before you think it's not for you, realize a disability is anything keeping you from work. This can be a bad sickness that causes you to be out of the office for several weeks. Or, if your job involves more labor intensive activities like working in a warehouse, a broken leg may keep you out for longer. It can even extend to a workplace accident (maybe you make heavy equipment like me) that permanently takes your ability to walk or use your hands.

You can get disability insurance in the marketplace, or you can look into getting it through your employer (normally cheaper this way). Talk to your Human Resources department to see what's available. In my case, my employer actually holds a short-term disability policy on each of its employees. It also makes long-term disability insurance available to employees if they want to make the extra purchase. Life is uncertain, so I invested in this.

17

RENTER'S INSURANCE

This is an easy one to overlook! Don't miss it! That is, unless you are a homeowner. Homeowners, please feel free to skip. For the rest of us renters, this is an important one.

"Yeah, Caleb, I get it. They're all important. Every single, stinking insurance you've listed is 'important.' Blah, blah, blah." Yeah, they kinda are. Anyway…

If you are a renter, your landlord is not responsible for losses of any of your belongings resulting from fire, flooding, theft, or whatever else. If your apartment or rental home burns down, you will get nothing. Obtain renter's insurance to avoid this. It'll cover anything from fire to theft. It's pretty easy to understand. Plus, it's not crazy expensive.

One thing to consider is that, many times, you can bundle up your insurances to get a better rate. For example, I don't have a house, but I am renting. The insurance company we use for vehicle insurance is the same that we use for our renter's insurance. That's a good way to save a couple bucks. Talk to your insurance professional to figure out if that's the best way to insure yourself and your stuff.

18

HOMEOWNER'S INSURANCE

Renter's insurance is very simple to understand; homeowner's insurance is slightly more complicated and confusing. Here's what you need to know.

When you purchase a home, there are a lot of upfront costs involved. For one, you've got closing costs. In addition to this, you have to prepay on your homeowner's insurance. Essentially, this takes care of the homeowner's insurance for the next year. Then, after the home is purchased, you will likely pay into a preset account every month in preparation for the next year of prepaid home insurance.

When it comes to home insurance, it's not as much a YOU-HAVE-TO-GET-THIS discussion because it is required by most mortgage companies in order to grant a mortgage to a buyer. The thing that may be a bigger consideration for you is whether or not to get flood insurance and/or earthquake insurance. Depending on your location in the country, you may be required by your mortgage company to get one or both of these. If you purchase a home located in a floodplain, you'll be required to get flood insurance. If you live close to a fault line, you may be required to get earthquake insurance. Again, talk to your insurance professional (and probably your realtor) to see if one or both of these insurances are something you should seriously consider.

If you purchase a home with cash (unlikely for a young person, but possible), that's when you may be tempted to skip homeowner's insurance, but you'll still need it. It'll cover large costs that you may not be able to swallow, even if you are debt-free. Like a hungry fire. Or a sneaky thief.

According to Nerd Wallet, one thing you should ask about your insurance is whether it replaces your belongings using replacement-cost coverage or actual-value coverage.[1] This is the difference between your things being replaced with brand new items or with

Insurance is so Confusing

items of similar value to your belongings. For example, I have a 2011, 21-inch iMac with a 2.7 GHz quad-core processor. If our imaginary house burned down with it in it (some of you are cheering because you are PC people…shame on you), the difference between replacing it with an iMac of similar value and a brand new iMac is at least $1000. Thus, your replacement-cost coverage is going to cost more.

RESOURCES

Check this out for more detailed information about homeowner's insurance: www.nerdwallet.com/blog/insurance/understanding-homeowners-insurance/

19

IDENTITY THEFT PROTECTION

Similar to health insurance, it's easy to be optimistic about your probability of needing identity theft protection. I know, insurance isn't in the name but that is what it is—an insurance policy.

I think it is especially important for young people to have identity theft protection because we are much more involved in online purchases and data. It's much easier to protect your identity as an elderly person if you hate all things technology and don't do anything with online accounts. The truth is, scams are everywhere, not only are they trying to take your money, but also your identity. If you aren't careful, identity thieves can take your money from savings accounts, retirement accounts, open credit card accounts, or even apply for loans in your name, like automobile financing.

Identity theft protection will monitor your credit report and contact you if there are purchases that are out of the ordinary or new accounts that have been opened. You can do that yourself, sure, but what would be much more difficult is trying to resolve all of the headache caused by identity theft yourself.

I always joke around about how nobody would want to steal my identity because no one wants to be me and I don't have enough that is worth stealing. But I do have identity theft protection (and so does Bailey). When you have identity theft protection, you don't have to worry (as much) about identity theft because you will have an advisor assigned to your case, helping resolve all the problems if a problem arises. It's worth the investment!

Insurance is so Confusing

RESOURCES
Here's a resource from Federal Trade Commission giving a bit more insight into protecting your identity:
www.consumer.ftc.gov/articles/0235-identity-theft-protection-services

20

A WORD ABOUT DEDUCTIBLES

"Deductible" remains one of the big words that gives me a headache when it comes to insurance. Gear up and take an aspirin because here's what you need to know. A deductible is essentially what you have to pay for a claim before your insurance company will pay any of the claim. Your monthly insurance payments will depend on what your deductible is. It's a give and take. If you have a lower deductible, your monthly payments will be higher and vice versa. Here's an example of how to understand deductibles.

This past December, I was being a mostly-law-abiding adult, driving to work at only 5 MPH over the speed limit when the vehicle ahead of me threw a rock up, cracking my windshield. We're not talking about a little crack. We're talking about a honking crack (pardon the car pun). This crack was, no exaggeration, three feet long. Needless to say, my entire windshield needed replaced. Bleh.

The thing was that my comprehensive (remember that term?) deductible for my car insurance was $250. The new windshield cost $252.52. So, in this case, I had to pay the entire amount because my insurance wasn't going to pay for anything until I had paid $250 first. I could have filled out a claim, but the most they would have paid would have been $2.52. Not exactly something worth fighting for.

When it comes to deductibles, for whatever insurance you have, you need to consider how high you want your deductible to be. How will you know? It'll depend on what your risk tolerance is, for one. It'll also depend on whether you have an emergency fund saved up (which we will cover more in the financial portion of this book). Generally speaking, if you have a full emergency fund saved, you can go with a higher deductible because you can cover a higher cost. But you will also save money on your monthly insurance payment.

Insurance is so Confusing

Something to consider: how long would it take to save (from monthly payments) the amount that it would take to cover the deductible you have? Let's look at another example.

Let's say your monthly payment for vehicle insurance was $100 and you had a $250 deductible. If you increased your deductible to $1000 but it only decreased your monthly payment by $12, it would take over five years to save up the difference between the two deductibles. That means you'd have to go over five years without making an insurance claim on your car before raising the deductible would make any sense.

However, if it saved you $25 a month, it would take you 30 months to save that back up. That's 2.5 years. Not bad if you are a safe driver.

RESOURCES

>Use this resource from Bank Rate to figure out generally what you want your insurance deductible to be: www.bankrate.com/finance/insurance/how-to-choose-insurance-deductible.aspx

PART VI

FINANCING MY LIFE

This section has turned out to be some of the most beneficial information for me to learn post-graduation. As I neared my departure from campus, I realized I would make more money than I had ever made before and that I needed a plan for it. I became fascinated with money information and advice. I obsessively read articles, watched videos and listened to podcasts. I learned about some great and powerful tools. I learned about mistakes other people made that I could avoid. Some of these things I have actually experienced and some I have only learned about. Regardless, this will give a brief overview of what you need to know and resources you can go to in order to learn more.

A quick note before getting into this delicate topic: I'm a Dave Ramsey fan and I have been for a while (obviously from all the quotes I have from him in this book). The reason I am a fan is because I have spent countless hours listening to his podcasts, following his advice, and hearing stories of hope by people every day who have pulled themselves out of utterly horrendous amounts of debt. I've seen his plan work. It's contrary to the way much of the world thinks and teaches about money. Sometimes, it doesn't mathematically make sense when talking about paying off debt in specific ways. However, his advice works and has worked for millions of people (literally *millions* have paid off debt based on his principles).

Thus, a large amount of financial advice in this book comes from the perspective of someone who's working through the Ramsey plan. If you don't agree, so be it, but I'll try to give as much reason behind everything as possible so you can understand the process to the best of your ability. Let's get into it!

21

BUDGET (DID YOU FALL ASLEEP YET?)

"So do you have a budget?" I asked. My friend looked up slightly, smiled and answered, "Kinda. I mean, I pay my bills every month so I use that as a way for me to see where my money is going at least."

I suspect this is the way many people answer this question. But this isn't budgeting. Budgeting is by far the most important piece of your finances. It is the tool that will contain your impulsiveness and give you freedom in the end! Trust me, I know this from experience. Now, there's something that needs to be cleared up when it comes to income and a budget. *It doesn't matter how much you make, you need to have a budget.* You may be a college student with loans to pay off; you need a budget. You may be an individual living in Silicon Valley leading a successful startup (which would greatly surprise me if you are reading my book); you also need a budget.

If there is anything in the financial realm that I have learned, it is that your money needs a plan. And the budget is that plan! When your money doesn't have a plan, it will go to anything. You may not be an impulsive buyer, but when you don't have a plan, you can justify anything. John Maxwell says, "A budget is telling your money where to go instead of wondering where it went." Now *that* is a plan.

Everything goes back to the budget. There are people who have won the lottery or played in the NFL with multimillion-dollar contracts and are currently broke because they didn't have a plan for their money. The ones who do have a plan are still doing well. Eddie George, the legendary Heisman Trophy winner (Go Bucks!) and NFL running back, said in an interview that immediately after signing a contract for the NFL, he began contributing to retirement and savings (George).[1] Again, that's a plan and it worked.

Let's do this.

Financing My Life

Budgeting sounds kind of intimidating, doesn't it? Some people think it's a swear word and never speak it. It's really not that hard to make one. Trust me! All you need is your bank statement and paper to start. Go through your bank statement and put your purchases into nine categories: Income, Giving, Saving, Housing, Transportation, Food, Lifestyle, Insurance, and Debt. Then, as you go through your bank statement for the last month, put each purchase and transaction into one of these categories. Charge for gas? Put it in Transportation. Charge for seeing a movie at the local theater? Put it in Lifestyle. Got paid this last Friday? Put it in Income. By doing this, you'll have each purchase in a category and it will give you a feel for where your money is going.

Now, the trick is not just making sure that your expenses are below your income for that month; the trick is making sure that every dollar that comes in has a plan for where to go. That means if you have any income that doesn't have a place, it should go towards savings or debt. Don't leave any money confused about where it should go because I guarantee that you will justify another place for it (*cough cough* restaurants).

It's probably going to take you at least three months to really get a good feel for the accuracy of your budget. It took Bailey and me about that long to feel very comfortable with the numbers we were projecting before the beginning of the next month.

There are several tools that can help you in making a budget. Some people like Microsoft Excel and there are plenty of spreadsheets already set up online to help you make a budget for the first time and control your money. Other people like the old-fashioned (and still relevant) pen and paper—though a pencil would probably be more appropriate in this case because you *will* be changing numbers, so have an eraser handy, too. Finally, some people like to have a budgeting app on their phones that allow them to keep track of their finances on the go. These are some great options:

<u>Microsoft personal budget template:</u> If you don't have it already, you can find it at <u>templates.office.com</u>. This is a very intuitive template that sets up initial categories and possible numbers for things like housing, utilities, and groceries.

<u>EveryDollar:</u> This is my personal favorite and what gets my endorsement. This is an app you can get on the App Store for iPhone

Graduated and Clueless

or on the Play Store for Android. This allows you to keep track of purchases on the go, which I find is very helpful. But the nice thing is that you can also use this software online, not just on the app. With my EveryDollar account, I can keep track on my app, then look at and modify my budget on my laptop as well. You can find the software at everydollar.com. I have found that it is very simple to use and makes it incredibly easy to set up your first budget. It also allows you to place funds in different categories. For example, if you are saving $25 a month for tires (like I am), it'll show you every month how much you have saved in that category altogether.

Ynab: This is another great app that you can get from either app store. You can access it online at ynab.com. Although it is intuitive, it will cost you a small fee every month. I don't use it because I didn't get started on it, so it was easier for me to continue on EveryDollar. However, this has many of the same features EveryDollar does.

Intuit Mint: Another app. And if you are into using TurboTax and Intuit's other software for taxes or business purposes, this may be a great option for you. You can get the app or find it at mint.com. And it's free!

The key to finding a budgeting system is that you need to choose one that is relatively simple, especially if you aren't a numbers person. The worst thing you can do for yourself is overcomplicate your finances. I say this from personal experience. This is why I started using EveryDollar. It was based on an account, so I could access it from my phone and my computer, which made it much more convenient. In addition to that, the categories it set up for me made the whole act of budgeting so much simpler.

Donald Miller writes in his bestselling book *Building a Storybrand* about how the human brain tunes out whatever causes it to burn too many calories (9). This was written in the context of building a clear business message, but is just as relevant in budgeting.

If you make budgeting too complicated, your brain will burn too many calories and you will not budget. So don't overcomplicate. Make it so that you can keep track but don't have to expel too much mental energy to make it happen. A budget will transform your finances. I guarantee it!

One last thing on budget: You have to *stick to it*. Not only do you need to create a budget every month before the month begins, you

Financing My Life

have to stick to your budget religiously. It can't be just a guideline for you, just showing you where your money should go. You have to plan your month so that you don't exceed your restaurant fund. From experience, I can say that is a difficult thing. If you know Christmas is coming (December 25th if you didn't), you can plan in your budget how you will save for it each month. A budget, if followed properly, will give you so much freedom. It actually makes Bailey and me feel like it's okay to spend money on ourselves because we budgeted spending money each month. And it's keeping us on track for our savings goals.

RESOURCES

EveryDollar: www.everydollar.com

Ynab: www.ynab.com

Intuit Mint: www.mint.com

22

YOU NEED AN EMERGENCY FUND

Similar to the budget, you need an emergency fund. As great as the budget is, it won't fully protect you in the event of an emergency. You always need an emergency fund. If you are in debt, Dave Ramsey suggests a $1000 emergency fund so that you can focus all the rest of your money on paying down debt. It's not much, but it develops an urgency to pay down debt as quickly as possible.

After having paid down debt to nothing, you will need to build a three- to six-month emergency fund and then not touch it. This is going to have to happen after you work on your budget. Obviously, you can save but you'll have to do some research into your budget to see what the absolute minimum is that you can live on every month. Then, depending on your comfort level with the amount of savings you have, save three to six times that amount into a savings account where you can access it quickly in the event of an emergency.

What's an emergency? That's a valid question. It's super easy to stretch the definition of an emergency when it comes to using your money. If you aren't careful, you'll justify any purchase as an emergency. Did your vehicle transmission break down on you today? That's an emergency. Did you have an unexpected medical expense? Again, a valid emergency. Did you forget about Christmas coming up? That is not an emergency.

The question to ask yourself is this: is the purchase I am about to make predictable? If the answer is yes, then it is not an emergency. That is where your budget comes in. If it's predictable, you need to have a line item in your budget for saving for that item. Plan ahead and you normally won't feel the need to dip into your emergency fund!

23

LOANS

Everyone's got a loan, right?

The truth is, the majority of millionaires believe that avoiding debt at all cost is the way to build wealth. I find it entertaining that a large chunk of Americans believe that debt is the way to get ahead, whereas the majority of millionaires—the ones who actually got to millionaire status—don't. Basically, you need to pay off any debt as quickly as is humanly possible.

Dave Ramsey is one of the leading financial voices in America, running the top privately-owned radio talk show in the nation (third rated talk show overall). He has helped millions through his financial radio advice and through his books. He has an unprecedented record for individuals he has helped destroy debt and reach financial freedom. You may not agree with his approach, but I believe that it is an effective way to build wealth, so that's what I'll outline here.

In his book *The Total Money Makeover*, Dave gives his baby steps to building wealth.[1] Step one involves saving a $1000 emergency fund. The second step is to pay off debt as quickly as possible. That just goes to show the importance of gaining financial freedom from other people. I mean, it's the second step overall. It's gotta be important, right? Dave doesn't believe that there is a "fast track" to becoming wealthy and his plan says that paying off debt is the fastest, most predictable way there is. In his book and other resources, he uses the analogy of a gazelle evading the capture of a jaguar for motivating his readers and listeners to destroy debt. He encourages people to attack and outrun debt like a gazelle, barely outrunning the claws of a ferocious cat.

Dave Ramsey says, "Your greatest financial tool is your income." When you have debt, the best tool you have is your own biweekly paycheck. If you have a lot of debt, increase your income. Get another job. Get a side hustle. Work overtime. Do whatever it takes. Can you

Graduated and Clueless

imagine not having a car payment? Or a student loan? When you aren't paying off loans, it increases the amount of your income you can put to things you value more. If you pay off your car loan, it means the next month you can put even more down on your house payment. Paying off debt just keeps working on itself and increases the speed at which you reach financial freedom.

Speaking of debt, when it comes to cars, generally speaking, it's wise to go with a used car around two years old. Within two years, the car has lost the greatest amount of value while retaining its greatest life potential. Go with a car that you don't have to get financed because interest you pay, once again, will significantly decrease your wealth-building potential.

According to Value Penguin, a company dedicated to helping individuals understand information on insurance and finances, the average credit score in America is 695.[2] With that score and a loan for a $20,000 car over a 5-year period, an individual would pay $22,618 in all for that car. That's 13% more than if they paid for it with cash. That's just the average. If you have a low credit score, say below 600, you'll be paying about 14.06% interest or more according to Value Penguin.[3] Over a 5-year period for the same $20,000 car, you would pay $27,959 for the car. That's nearly 40% more than what the car was worth when you paid for it!

In as much as you can, do everything possible with cash. Don't purchase things that you can't afford. According to Ramsey, the only circumstance in which it is acceptable to use a loan is in obtaining a house. That is outlined more fully in the housing chapter.

After the last couple of chapters, I hope that you see the significance of interest. It is a huge part of our society and can greatly damage your overall saving ability. But one thing I'd like you to realize is this: you can be on either end of interest. You can make it work against you. Or, as you'll see with retirement, you can make it work for you in significant ways.

Financing My Life

RESOURCES

Value Penguin on average credit scores: www.valuepenguin.com/average-credit-score

Value Penguin on auto loan interest rates:
www.valuepenguin.com/auto-loans/average-auto-loan-interest-rates

24

NOW YOU'VE GOT BILLS!

Oh bills, what a joy! Dave Ramsey said that when his kids moved out at their respective times, something changed in them. They walked differently and stood taller because they had greater responsibilities post-move-out. They were paying their own bills.

If you have a checking account and an internet connection, this section is going to be very simple for you. All you need to do is set up all your bills for automatic payments. Some people are afraid of setting up automatic payments because they're afraid they won't see if there's a problem with a bill. I, however, find them incredibly convenient. Not only do I not have to worry about making a late payment, but I also don't have to spend an evening every month signing onto my accounts and making bill payments if I'm not sending checks. And honestly, I don't think I can remember all my passwords.

You may feel more comfortable getting the bill and making the payment yourself. I'm sure it has psychological benefits to it, considering that you see the amount and actually have to hit the "Pay Now" button. A friend of mine doesn't do automatic payments because it's a way for him to keep up with what he's spending. But for me, automatic payments make my life easy (okay, okay, easier). I still check my checking account regularly and get the bills emailed to me every month so that I can see what I'm paying. I recommend doing this so you still have an understanding of where your money gets absorbed, but change to automatic payments and you'll save a boatload of time!

25

TAXES, BLEH!

They say that there are only two things you can be sure of in this world: death and taxes. We already covered life insurance for if you die—now let's cover the second one! In my survey, I found many people were interested in learning more about taxes and not being clueless about them. This will be my attempt at helping you feel more comfortable about the subject.

TAX WITHHOLDINGS

No one likes taxes. Well, ok, the government and schools do. That's about it. But I haven't ever met anyone who actually likes being taxed. However, what I'm going to say next, you may not like much. Taxes are actually our contribution to this great country that we live in (assuming that you live in the United States of America)! They provide us safety through the military and police and fire departments. They benefit us in infrastructure through roads, bridges, and other forms of transportation. And, they keep us socially structured. That way we don't resort to anarchy. Taxes actually do a lot of good.

Having said that, I am a capitalist, so I believe that not everything should be provided through the government (i.e. health care). So I don't like high taxes and I don't like the government using my money inefficiently, hence my dislike of the subject. But it's a fact of life, so we'll cover it.

When you graduate and get a job (if you are not self-employed), your employer will automatically withhold a certain amount of your paycheck and send it to the IRS (Internal Revenue Service). Taxes are withheld to keep you from getting to tax season and realizing you don't have enough to pay the government. This, I can imagine, is a horrible feeling. Thank goodness for tax withholding!

Your employer will give you something called a W-4 IRS form. This form, when you fill it out, will let the government know how much

Graduated and Clueless

should be withheld depending on your life situation. If you are married, you'll put that down on the form. If you have kids, you'll also put that down. Then, depending on what you put on the form, a certain percentage of your paycheck will be withheld and sent to the IRS.

When tax season rolls around, you fill out some forms and the government (hopefully) sends you a refund check, assuming they withheld too much of your paycheck. This can be a great feeling! It's like a huge paycheck that you get without doing anything. But here's something you might not realize: *that was all your money in the first place.*

When you allow the government to take more of your money than they need to throughout the year, you are essentially giving an interest-free loan to the government. Albert Einstein once said that those who have debt pay interest, but those who don't will get interest. Why are you letting the government keep your money interest-free? You could put the money from your refund check into a savings account throughout the year and you'd have more than you got back from the government. And if you put that into your retirement account, you'd (likely) have even more money.

This is what you need to do: adjust your withholdings so that when you complete your taxes during tax season, you get as close to $0 back from the government as possible. This doesn't feel as good because you don't get a big refund check back from the government. But it does mean that you got more back in each paycheck throughout the year, allowing you to put it to savings, retirement, or maybe a house payment. You certainly don't want to have too little withheld from your paycheck. I don't want you to get to tax season and owe the government even more. But you do want to be as close to a $0 refund as possible.

This is where you need to get together with a Human Resources individual at your workplace and ask them to help you find where that healthy medium is. You may have to talk to a tax professional so that they can take your life circumstances into consideration (home-ownership, spouse, kids, etc.) and help you figure out how much you need withheld. You may have to experiment a bit. I have. This year, Bailey and I got a larger refund than expected. Thus, I got together

Financing My Life

with HR at work and changed my W-4 form so that it withholds less than the previous year.

Let's say you got a $700 refund. You change your W-4 form so that it withholds less this year than last. In the next paycheck, you notice that you got $25 more. If you get paid every other week then you would get

$25 per paycheck x 26 paychecks per year = $650

This would work very well because you would then (theoretically) get a $50 refund the next year, assuming nothing changed with your job. Then you can get interest back on that $650 from a savings or retirement account.

City taxes are also withheld from your paycheck if you work in a city. For me, I work in one city and live in another. Unfortunately, that means I pay taxes in both cities. Only the city I work in withholds taxes from my paycheck. This means that I have to consciously save what I think I will owe in taxes to the city in which I live. Consider this as you get your taxes in order depending on where you live.

TAX PREPARATION

Tax season is very confusing. Should you try to do your taxes yourself or should you pay someone to do them for you? It really depends, in my opinion. Many people our age don't have complicated taxes, which leaves them many options for tax preparation. Online tax-preparation software like TurboTax is a good option. I like these types of software because they ask you fairly simple questions in order to get you the largest refund possible. There are also many reasonably priced tax-preparation companies with which you can get your taxes completed in less than an hour. Then, of course, there's the old-fashioned fill-out-the-physical-form-and-mail-it-to-the-IRS-yourself option.

However, for people with more complicated taxes, you may want to hire a tax professional that can get into more tax details depending on your situation. I suggest this especially for those people who have many streams of income (ride-sharing, side business, etc.). I will personally be doing this next year. I have a normal job as an engineer and I have a business. Bailey, last year, worked for three different

Graduated and Clueless

companies at different times. Needless to say, I spent an unbelievable amount of time on preparing our taxes and I hated all of it. I value my time more than the money I would save and next year, I will pay a professional do it.

If you have a bunch of complicated things that affect taxes, I would get a professional to prepare your taxes because there's a higher likelihood that you'll get as large a refund as possible, even though you have to pay the preparer. Plus, you'll be able to use your time more wisely than on taxes. But if you only have one job, you're renting your apartment, and you aren't in school anymore, tax preparation may be simple enough to do yourself. And you'll save a few bucks.

26

SHOULD I GIVE MY HARD-EARNED MONEY AWAY?

How do you view the word generosity? Charity? Non profits? For me, since I'm a Christian, it mostly means giving to my church and to Christian organizations I believe will use the money I give wisely and for God's kingdom. To those who aren't Christians, see title below.

For Christians, the key is in understanding from where your money comes. I believe God has blessed me and Bailey with more than we need to live. It's all His money; we are merely stewards (caretakers) of His money. Randy Alcorn, a leading voice on the Biblical interpretation of eternity, said this in his excellent book, *The Treasure Principal,* "Suppose you have something important you want to get to someone who needs it. You wrap it up and hand it over to the FedEx guy. What would you think if instead of delivering the package, he took it home, opened it, and kept it for himself?" (76). That's essentially how it is when we take our paycheck and pretend as if it doesn't belong to God in the first place. That's why we give a tithe. As a matter of faith, Bailey and I give God 10% of our income for His work through our church based on the tithe outlined in the Bible. We also give offerings (which is above the tithe) to our church and to missions.

God blesses through our giving. Not necessarily monetarily as many "health and wealth" preachers teach. I believe He blesses us spiritually with more faith. When we give, especially when we don't think we have enough to give, God reminds us in whom we need to put our trust. He says in Matthew 6:21, "For where your treasure is, there your heart will be also." Where do you put your treasure? In the materialism of this life or in Jesus?

This is one of my greatest weaknesses. When I was young, my money burned a hole in my pocket whenever I had some. If we went to the grocery store, I would occasionally get a pack of gum just for the dopamine rush it gave me to spend some major coin (ok, it was major for me in that day). It seriously took me all year to save $20 as a kid and I usually spent a good chunk of that at Christmas. Now, it's not packs of gum but it is other things like electronics. I like computers, tablets, phones, drones, and anything else that rhymes and has a microchip. One of my past times is to research new camera equipment because I like filmmaking.

The point is, I am very materialistic at times. It takes me being very intentional to remember where it comes from and that none of it lasts. I have to pray and ask God that I would hold everything that I have with open hands. That way He can take what I have if that is His will. And yet, He can also give me more or better things when my hands are open. Whether it is my electronics, my car or even my relationships, I have to remember who grants me these blessings.

The nice thing is, God rewards those who are His redeemed children and give for His kingdom by preparing treasures for them in Heaven. (Matthew 6:20). This doesn't mean if we give here on Earth, we will only reap small rewards while we live. In fact, in Mark 10:29-30, Jesus says that if you give up all that you have for Him and for the gospel, you will reap one hundred times what you sowed. That's a lot of harvest agriculturally speaking! There is so much more to be said on the topic but here is the point: Your salvation is not dependent on what you do or what you give. It is only dependent on the precious blood of Jesus Christ. Giving is just an outward showing of our faith to God (and has its own eternal rewards).

"WHAT IF I'M NOT A CHRISTIAN? HOW DOES GIVING AFFECT ME?"

If you aren't a Christian, I can't use the eternal impact of giving as motivation because you don't have that worldview. However, I can say this: statistically, those who give consider themselves more thankful and lead happier lives according to Science Daily.[2] They say, "In their experiments, the researchers found that people who behaved generously were happier afterwards than those who behaved more selfishly." People want to be happy in life. Even the most selfish individuals. At a minimum, isn't giving worth the return on investment in happiness, peace, and living a more grateful life?

Financing My Life

WHO SHOULD I GIVE MY MONEY TO?

Personally, Bailey and I like to give money to our church. We know where it is going because we have semiannual budget meetings. Also, we know that it is going to discipling people in their faith (which is incredibly important to us) and to reaching the people of our community for Christ. This also includes missionaries that our church supports. But we also give to Compassion International (www.compassioninternational.com) every month by "adopting" a child. This provides money for food, clothing and educational needs (as well as biblical teaching) to children in poverty-stricken countries. However, we also occasionally give to friends or family involved in fundraisers for things like cancer research.

These organizations are important to us. Specifically because they have eternal impact on many people. What good causes are important to you? Where you give must have some personal meaning to you.

The thing about giving is that you get to show what's important to you with your money. When you put your money where your mouth is, people will take you more seriously, even if they don't believe in the cause or organization. I know that I do. Even if you don't consider yourself religious, this is one reason giving will help you.

Here's one word of warning. Not all nonprofits are created equal. Being nonprofit only means that the organization is not doing business for profit. The CEO could literally be making millions and very little may be going to the purposes you thought. Keep this in mind. Find organizations you like that have a high percentage of donations going to their mission statement.

RESOURCES:

Science Daily on the relationship of happiness and generosity:
www.sciencedaily.com/releases/2017/07/170711112441.htm

PART VII

GOOD, OLD RETIREMENT

....

Bailey's grandfather has been a farmer his whole life. A couple years ago, he and his wife semi-retired. They sold most of the farm and moved to the nearby, small town. Now he does a little farming with the remaining land for the heck of it and goes into the "office" everyday because he can. The "office" is how he refers to where he and his retired friends drink coffee and play cards every morning. You know why he can do this? Because he's been saving for retirement.

This is not a big section, but it is a very important one. It's just as important (if not more so) for us millennials as it is for every other age! Retirement planning, though, is especially difficult for young people because it's so easy to focus on the here and now, not worrying about your money 40 years from now. I mean, come on, you need a new phone *now* (please don't finance it)!

But here is where delayed gratification comes into play. This is the definition for delayed gratification, straight from Wikipedia:

Delayed gratification, or deferred gratification, is the ability to resist the temptation for an immediate reward and wait for a later reward.

If you save now, you'll have more later. If you take advantage of retirement savings when you're young, it'll make an exponential difference! That is how compounded interest works. For those of you who don't know, compounded interest is where you gain interest on interest. So if you put $1000 into an account at 10% interest, the first year, you will get $100 from interest. Then you'll have $1100 in your account. The next year, you'll get $110 from interest because you are gaining 10% interest on your $1000 and 10% interest on your $100. And it keeps growing from there.

Albert Einstein said, "Compound interest is the eighth wonder of the world. He who understands it, earns it ... he who doesn't ... pays it." If you are saving for retirement, you're earning compound interest. If

Graduated and Clueless

you have debt, you're paying compound interest. So make it work for you.

There are a few things to realize when you are investing for retirement. Investing is generally considered investing only if it is held in one place for more than five years. In the case of 401(k)s and IRAs, the money will be held in the account for closer to 40 years or more if you start investing at a young age. Now, that is an investment.

In his book, *Retire Inspired*, Chris Hogan describes investing as a roller coaster. He says this: "Parts of the ride may be fun, and other parts may scare you to death. But if you hold on and see the ride through to the end, you usually come out just fine. But if you try to jump off early, well, you are going to get hurt" (100). Your investment roller coaster will go up and it'll feel good for the time being. It will go down, though, and when it does, you just have to grip the handlebars and keep riding. Because the only people who get hurt on a roller coaster are the ones who jump off.

Buy low, sell high. That's what the experts say. When your investments go down, don't get worried, just ride it out to the end and you won't get hurt! In the next chapters, we'll look at retirement savings.

Retirement is something you would be wise to seek professional advice concerning. Keep in mind, investment firms have fees attached to managing your money. If you aren't careful who you work with, the fees may be a large chunk of your rate of return, decreasing your earning potential. Ramsey Solutions has a list of trusted investment professionals where you can find a professional in your area.

RESOURCES

Investment Professionals: www.daveramsey.com/smartvestor?ictid=tp.nav&snid=recommends.smartvestor

# 27

WHAT IS A 401(K)?

I used to hear that combination of numbers and letters thrown around on a regular basis, but what is it? All you really need to know is that a 401(k) is a retirement savings plan that everyone should take advantage of. Here's how it works if you set it up at your place of employment.

1. A portion of every paycheck that you receive is automatically taken out and placed into an account that will grow exponentially with time.
2. This account is only available to you penalty-free if you wait until you are 59 1/2 years of age to take any money out.
3. Based on your place of employment, you will likely receive an additional percentage of your paycheck deposited into your 401(k) account by your employer as a benefit. Most of the time, this is between 3 and 10% of your paycheck. This is free money that is given to you by your employer.

Do you understand that? Look again. Literally, if you put money into your 401(k), your employer will match your deposit up to a certain percentage. Again, that is FREE money! It's a big deal. If your employer will match your contribution to your 401(k) up to 5%, you need to take full advantage of it. So you need to contribute at least 5% of your paycheck each pay period. Here's an example.

Your paycheck: $1000. If you contribute 5%, you will be putting $50 into your 401(k) for retirement. Your employer will also put in 5% ($50). Every pay period, you are putting $100 into your retirement savings by only putting in half of it!

There are two types of 401(k)s. There is the traditional 401(k) and the Roth 401(k). Your contribution to a traditional 401(k) will be tax free, but you will pay taxes on what you pull out of your account when

Graduated and Clueless

you retire. If you have a Roth 401(k), however, your contributions will be taxed, but the money you withdraw from it at retirement will be tax free. Here's another example.

Traditional 401(k)
Paycheck: $1000. Taxes: 20%.
Thus, you pay $200 in taxes. However, if you contribute 10% ($100) into your 401(k), your paycheck will be $900. Then 20% of $900 is $180, leaving $720 for you to save or spend.

Roth 401(k)
Paycheck: $1000. Taxes: 20%.
You pay $200 in taxes, which leaves you $800 before your 401(k) contribution. 10% ($100) into your 401(k) will leave you with $700 to save or spend.

Now, do you see what happened in the example? In the traditional 401(k), your contribution is made and then your taxes are taken out, leaving you $720. In the Roth 401(k), taxes are taken out and then your contribution is made, leaving you $700. The difference is that when you retire, you will have to pay taxes on the traditional 401(k), including the growth of the account. With the Roth 401(k), you pay taxes on only what is put in (the contributions). Thus, when you retire, you get to pull the money out without having to pay a dime to the government. By taking $20 less in your paycheck now, you'll pay nothing on the *$1.1 million* you would earn from investing $100 of each paycheck at 10% interest for 40 years. If you use the traditional 401(k), you would pay the government a hefty sum of the $1.1 million.

The only thing you'll have to pay taxes on from Roth is the amount your employer matched and its growth. The short and sweet of this paragraph is this: Roth is better. Choose the Roth if your employer offers it.

The last thing you really need to know about 401(k)s is that you are permitted to contribute up to $18,500 per year. No more. Now, that's not going to be a problem for the majority of you (including me), but given the benefits, that is the maximum currently allowed by the U.S. government.

28

IRA (MORE LETTER COMBINATIONS)

The individual retirement arrangement (also known as the IRA) is another excellent way to prepare for retirement. Similar to the 401(k), there is a traditional IRA and a Roth IRA. Additionally similar to the 401(k), the traditional IRA is a pre-tax account and the Roth IRA is a post-tax account.

Unlike the 401(k), the IRA is not offered by employers. Almost anyone can open an IRA and contribute to it whenever they want. In the case of the IRA, the maximum contribution you can make is $5500 per year (and per spouse if you're married). Once again, the Roth is a much better choice for those who still have a lot of time left before retirement.

If and when you change jobs, do a direct rollover of your 401(k) to a Roth IRA. Have money saved, though, because if it is a traditional 401(k), you will have to pay taxes on the entire amount. If it's a Roth 401(k), you will only have to pay taxes on the employer match. Doing the direct rollover to a Roth IRA allows the money in your 401(k) to grow fully tax-free until the day of your retirement.

29

STOCKS

Many people have their retirement savings in individual stocks. The problem with this strategy is that it isn't very diversified. When I talk about "diversification," I'm talking about ensuring that not all your eggs are in one basket. If you don't diversify and you drop the basket, you're out of luck. Better heat up the griddle pretty quick.

Stocks are not diversified because they are individual. If you buy one share of Facebook stock for $217 and that day Facebook stock jumps 20% (unlikely but possible), you have made a seemingly good decision. The problem lies in that it can also just as easily drop 20% in a day. This literally happened just recently. Investors lost more than $100 billion combined in one day. The other problem with purchasing individual stocks is that it opens you up to your personal preferences. Do you have an affinity for heavy equipment and their respective companies? You might buy stock in John Deere, Case New Holland, Caterpillar, and Doosan Corporation (manufacturer of Bobcat). All these are equipment companies. It's important to realize that sometimes there are problems that may affect an entire industry. For instance, in the case of these four companies, if steel prices jump drastically, all four companies will be affected. You may have shares in several companies, but if a problem arises that affects the equipment industry, you can lose a significant amount of savings in a few days. This is why mutual funds will help diversify your savings into not only different companies but also different industries.

Let me get something clear. Diversification is not buying individual stock from 10 companies. That's really not changing your risk levels much. However, mutual funds are an excellent way of diversifying your portfolio. We'll discuss this in the next chapter.

30

MUTUAL FUNDS

The term "mutual fund" was one of the most confusing things for me to understand about investing, so I don't blame you if the word combination intimidates you! Here's what you need to know: mutual funds exist to help people mitigate risk.

Essentially, a mutual fund is made up of a bunch of people putting their money into one big pot in order to purchase a variety of company stocks, normally between 90 and 200. Then, fund managers are paid a small fee in order to manage what companies the stocks are purchased in. This mitigates risk because, generally speaking, the average value of the mutual fund will rise. When you have single stocks, as mentioned in the previous chapter, you are at the mercy of how the market acts. If your Apple stock goes up, great! If your Amazon stock goes down, bummer.

When you are invested in mutual funds, you are still at the mercy of how the market acts, but you're diversified. If your Apple and Amazon stocks go up, but your Home Depot stock goes down, you likely will get a small increase in the value of your fund. This is a small example. If you look at the average of the 90 to 200 bits of company stock you own, you'll see they will generally produce an average of 7-10% interest. Then you don't have to deal with losing all your retirement savings in one day if one CEO makes a huge mistake!

Mutual funds are the main portion of your 401(k) or IRA. So when you put your money into your retirement account, a little bit is going to purchase a small part of a bunch of companies or bonds (another type of savings to be outlined in the following chapter). Then you get to watch it grow!

31

BONDS

A bond is a different kind of retirement savings and sometimes the mutual funds you choose for your 401k or IRA will have bonds in them to help balance the money you invest. These return a lower interest rate but tend to be a bit more predictable.

I don't currently have very much saved for retirement, so my 401(k) and IRA are made of a target-date fund. Basically, I choose when I will likely retire and the fund managers will put my money into a fund they have developed based on my age. This fund has a combination of stocks and bonds in them. Since I'm young, it will tend to be slightly higher risk since I have less to lose. However, as I get older, more and more of my money will be moved to bonds (if I don't change what mutual fund it is invested in) because they are more conservative, consistent, and predictable.

32

HOW MUCH SHOULD I INVEST?

"Ok, so I need to invest, I get it. But how much should I invest per month? And how much will I need for retirement?" These are excellent questions to ask because they get you to the specifics of investing. Let's use some examples to understand how this works within the context of you investing in a Roth 401(k).

First of all, the fourth "baby step" of the Ramsey plan is to put 15% of your gross income into retirement. That means 15% of your overall income, including your spouse's, goes into your 401(k) *after* paying off all your debt (so that you pay off debt with more intensity). Fifteen percent is generally agreed upon in the investing world to be the amount that will provide a reasonable retirement nest egg. However, depending on whose advice you're taking, this amount does not include the money that is contributed as an employer match. If your employer matches 5%, don't put yours at 10% and call it good. This way, the employer match will just be icing on the cake when you hit retirement. Now, 15% feels like a lot (it is, especially for young people). You will likely have to work your way up to it. Currently, Bailey and I aren't contributing 15% because we are also cash-flowing her school and are saving for a house. But 15% is the goal. Okay, let's move on to some examples.

Let's assume that you, at age 22, just graduated debt-free and your overall income is $50,000 per year. By the 15% rule, you would be putting $7500 into retirement per year ($625 per month). If you invested that at an 8% return and never got a raise (not likely), you would have $2,669,622 by the time you turned 65. The best part is that $2,347,122 was growth from interest! And that's not even including employer matches. That's remarkable!

That amount of contributions may be unrealistic for you. I know it is for us currently. If you could only afford $100 per month to put into your 401(k) at an 8% return and never increased the amount you

Graduated and Clueless

contributed, you would still have $427,139 by the time you turned 65. There is a very high likelihood that you will get a raise and that you'll be able to contribute more than $100 per month (plus, in today's money, $427k won't get you very far in retirement). To put you just over $1,000,000 (making you a millionaire), you would only have to contribute $250 per month. Again, your contributions would equal only a fraction of the full nest egg when you reached retirement. Then, in retirement, you will (hopefully) be able to live off of the yearly dividends that your retirement account produces in interest. On a $1,000,000 account, assuming 8% interest, that would provide an $80,000 income. Plus, it's quite possible to get higher than 8% in interest!

I hope that this puts into perspective the value of time when it comes to investing. This allows you to realize that it actually is possible to become a millionaire! Then, as Dave Ramsey would say, you can live and give like no one else.

RESOURCES

Here are a couple great resources that may aid you in your retirement plans.

1. Chris Hogan's book *Retire Inspired*.
2. Chris Hogan's website where you can figure out what your Retire Inspired Quotient (RIQ) is. This is the amount of money that you will theoretically need in retirement along with the amount that needs to be saved per month.
www.chrishogan360.com

PART VIII

DATING FOR THE MASSES

It's cool. If you skipped straight to this section of the book, I understand. I did that for many books I read before I got married as well. So here's the scoop: I didn't date around. That may make you want to quit reading this right now. I mean, how much dating advice can someone with "not much experience" truly give? Well, for one, Bailey and I dated for two years prior to marriage. So there's that. For two, I'm married. I sealed the deal. I tied the knot. Clearly something went right.

I understand, dating can be very complicated. There is a huge learning curve when you start spending serious time with someone of the opposite sex! I am going to lead you through (in a somewhat shallow-but-helpful way) Bailey's and my relationship as we moved towards marriage. My hope is that it will help you in the relationships you have and in your search for a life-long *married* partner.

33

NOT DATING YET? HERE'S HOW WE STARTED

The beginning of Bailey's and my relationship was a bit different from most people's relationships. For one, Bailey is almost exactly three years younger than me (only a day off). Because of that and our ages at the time, I wanted to go about this differently. I actually asked her dad, Vern, if it was okay with him if I asked her to date me.

Yes, I actually asked him first. He's a big guy, which contributed to this being the second most terrifying question I have ever posed to someone. The first was when I asked him for his blessing to marry his daughter.

After gaining his approval (to date), I had lunch with Bailey and I asked if she would date me. This was probably the third most terrifying question I've ever asked. After she approved, we were "officially" dating. This was super weird to me. I hadn't ever dated anyone before Bailey. I was learning how this thing worked.

This is by no means the way that I think everyone should do it. In fact, I could see myself doing it significantly differently under different circumstances. I think the important thing is having the relational intelligence to understand how to begin a dating relationship. Is the family of the individual you are considering more conservative or less so? Is dating or courting more appropriate in your case?

I recommend seeking out advice from trusted people about dating the individual you are considering. This is important, especially if your relationship looks promising long term. I talked individually with my dad, my sister, my youth director, and a close friend. I wanted honest opinions from several unique perspectives and I knew I could trust each of these individuals to give me advice. I talked to my dad because I wanted the advice from the man who taught me to become a man. I talked to my sister, Atalie, because I wanted advice from a

Dating for the Masses

female who also knew Bailey well. I talked to my youth director, Kevin, because he's a friend, a mentor, and because dating in the youth group would potentially affect his work. And lastly, I talked to my friend, Isaac, because he and I were in similar life situations. If you seek advice from several perspectives, it'll help you understand various opinions and different pros and cons.

Just don't stress it. Going on a date with someone doesn't mean you're exchanging vows later that evening. You don't even have to be officially dating. Just go out with them and see how it goes! In my case, I had known Bailey for three years before we started dating. Plus I had been around her in many situations and had seen how she interacted with and treated the people around her with respect. This is why I didn't feel the need to ask her on a single date beforehand. I already knew more about her than most people learn on their first five dates. The point is, this worked for me but your situation is more than likely different than mine.

Like I said, just go out with them. If they're crazy, it'll show up.

34

POINTS TO WORK THROUGH TOGETHER

Let's assume you are already dating.

Dating can be a touchy and confusing subject. People want a list of things they can do to guarantee a successful relationship. Unfortunately, it's not that easy. I don't have a list for you of what to do. However, I do have a list of some major considerations you should make and guidelines to follow when considering your significant other for marriage. Here is a short list of what you should think about:

1. What do they believe?
2. How does their character measure up?
3. Where are they going?

WHAT DO THEY BELIEVE?
This is the most significant thing you need to take into consideration. What does your significant other believe? With what worldview do they look at the world? If you don't marry someone who has similar views about God, spirituality, and the afterlife, there is likely going to be some major conflict in the future. "Living on love" isn't necessarily going to hold up.

For myself, I wouldn't marry anyone who wasn't a Christian. The reason is because Christ is such an integral part of my life. He is why I believe and act as I do about all aspects of life. He is the glasses through which I look at the world. The Bible says in 2 Corinthians 6:14 that we are not to be "unequally yoked with unbelievers." It seems pretty strict, but if you don't follow this, you could end up with some major heartache in the future.

"But I can affect them and change their heart and help them believe!" Yeah, and vice versa. It's just as easy for them to influence you as it is for you to influence them. If you have certain major beliefs you will not compromise, be wary of this mindset.

HOW DOES THEIR CHARACTER MEASURE UP?
Really, what do you see in their character after the newness of dating has worn off?

Are they mature?
Are they strong in their character?
Are they humble?
Are they honest?
Do they have a strong work ethic?
Are they loyal?
Are they trustworthy?

Character will show through after you've spent a lot of time together. An individual's guard will be let down after time has passed. When this happens, you can see someone's true colors. Ask others what their opinions of your significant other are. They won't be caught up in the emotions of dating and can more clearly look at the relationship from a reasonable perspective.

Character is important because it will affect all areas of life. From a Christian perspective, someone may be a Christian and believe many of the things that I believe about the world, but their character can be far from where it should be. Unfortunately, there are plenty of proud, untrustworthy, and immature Christians in the world. In addition to talking to others about their opinion of your significant other's character, talk to those you trust about the non-negotiable character traits your significant other must possess. You don't want to be married to someone you can't trust, no matter how hot they are.

WHERE ARE THEY GOING?
What are the goals of your significant other? Where do they see themselves going in the future? What do they want to do for a long-term career? Do they want a family? What personal development goals do they want to complete? What things are they passionate about? In what organizations do they want to get involved?

Look at the goals you and your significant other have. Do they align? If you want a family, but your significant other has more goals involving their career path, it may result in many late nights at the office for them and frustrating evenings alone with the kids for you.

Graduated and Clueless

You have to be going in the same direction if you move forward with marriage. It will keep much heartache from not only you, but also from your future spouse.

CAN I GET A TEST DRIVE (SEXUALLY)?

Personally, I wouldn't recommend this. It won't result in the best relationship you can have in the future. When you "test drive" your significant other sexually before you've tied the knot, it will change how you look at your relationship. You may begin to seek the benefits without the commitment. What's wrong with that? Studies show it results in a decrease in sexual satisfaction in marriage.[1] Not to mention, if it doesn't work out with your significant other, you'll have that emotional baggage to carry into marriage with a different individual.

Sex is meant for emotional connection and physical needs. That is how God designed it. And He specifically said in Hebrews 13:4 (NIV), "Marriage should be honored by all, and the marriage bed kept pure, for God will judge the adulterer and all the sexually immoral." If you use it outside of the confines of marriage, there will be consequences. It'll affect you emotionally, physically, and spiritually. If you wait, it'll make your marriage that much stronger.

Unfortunately, waiting on sex until marriage won't automatically make sex easy and wonderful. It still takes work. Take it from someone who knows! But by God's grace, you'll grow closer to each other through it and you'll experience an emotional connection that only a married couple should understand.

WHAT IF I'VE BEEN TEST DRIVING?

I would suggest you stop and develop some boundaries that you both agree upon. From personal experience, I can say physical boundaries can be incredibly difficult to incorporate into your relationship. But they are vital if you want to help your probability of staying with your significant other through a long and satisfying marriage. If you've been test driving over and over, you may need to ask a trusted friend to act as an accountability partner in this. Accountability is what Alcoholics Anonymous use because it works.

The important thing is to know that there is grace for the broken. God will forgive this sin if you ask Him to! He can redeem you from

Dating for the Masses

sexual sin just as He can from any other sin. But if you do, you have to change your ways!

WHAT ABOUT LIVING TOGETHER?
Once again, I wouldn't recommend it. There is far too much temptation involved in living together, even if you aren't deliberately having sex. It doesn't make sense sexually, but it also doesn't make sense financially and practically. When you're married, your assets are combined. What if you're living together but one of you leaves? You may suddenly be saddled with debt or a rent (or even a house) payment that you can't afford. When you live together, once again, there's no commitment involved and it's far too easy to get screwed over.

WHAT IF WE'RE ALREADY LIVING TOGETHER?
I'd recommend you get married as soon as possible. Don't wait a year so you have the perfect venue or the right photographer. That or move out. If you've answered the questions above and have concluded this isn't the right person for you to marry, don't prolong things.

RESOURCES
In these articles, you can see some of the research behind premarital sex and the ways it affects the likelihood of divorce:

> Institute for Family Studies: www.ifstudies.org/blog/counterintuitive-trends-in-the-link-between-premarital-sex-and-marital-stability

Focus on the Family: www.focusonthefamily.com/about/focus-findings/marriage/premarital-sex-and-divorce

PART IX

ADD MARRIAGE ON TOP OF ALL THIS

I graduated on May 7, 2017, started working full time on the 15th (come on, gotta have a week for vacation, right?), then I moved out and got married just a month later. Change is a healthy thing but this much change all at once? Come on. It can add quite a bit of stress to a new marriage if not prepared for in advance. So that's what we'll talk about here.

You may think that this does not apply to you if you aren't engaged, but it probably does. Statistically, you are likely to get married at some point in your life. This will focus more on those who have gotten married or are considering it soon after college, but it can be equally applicable to anyone who reads this.

Bailey and I began dating in December of 2014. It was a big step for both of us because neither of us had ever had an "official" relationship. Over the next two years, we developed a very strong relationship. We went to church together. We went on dates. We read relationship books together. On our two-year dating anniversary (affectionately known as our "dateversary"), I asked her to be my wife. This was, by far, the most significant question I had ever asked anyone. Between our engagement and the wedding stood one final semester of college for me. I graduated, we got married, and we started life together with far more changes at once than either of us had ever experienced.

What I found was that preparing for marriage wasn't like anything I had prepared for in the past. Not like college. Not like vacation. And it certainly wasn't anything like preparing for a campout with the cousins (for one, there are fewer airsoft battles in marriage). Go figure? Fortunately, we did prepare and I'll share our experiences here.

35

PREPARING FOR MARRIAGE

Our six months before marriage involved several different means of preparation. Marriage counseling was a big one for us, and it proves to be one of the most important based on marriage research. An article on WebMD.com outlines that couples who go through marital counseling before tying the knot have a 30% higher likelihood of having a stronger marriage than couples who don't.[1] That's huge. Of course, this doesn't mean that you won't have a good marriage if you skip counseling beforehand, but why wouldn't you take the opportunity to increase your chances by 30% given the opportunity?

Find a pastor or an older couple that you trust and ask if you can meet with them regularly to learn about everyday marriage. Discuss the harder topics. The key is to find people to conduct the counseling who aren't afraid to ask the tough questions. I know from experience that it's easy to develop a rose-colored view of your future spouse, which is even more reason for you to discuss everything.

Another big preparation technique for Bailey and me was reading relationship books together over our dating period. When we went on dates, especially if we were driving anywhere (which was almost all the time), whoever wasn't driving would read from a book we had agreed upon to help us in preparation for marriage. That's right, we read marriage books when we were dating. And I wouldn't have had it any other way.

One of the books we read was *The Mingling of Souls* by Matt Chandler. This was a good read that broke down marriage into the main categories and gave practical wisdom and advice based on Matt's marriage. Another great book we read (more like discussed) was *101 Questions to Ask Before You Get Engaged* by H. Norman Wright. I'll be honest, when we started this one, I didn't tell Bailey what the title was. I was kind of afraid it would scare her because it was earlier on in our relationship, before we had discussed marriage

Add Marriage on Top of All This

much. But was I thinking about marriage at that time? Ohhhh, yes. Most definitely. This was another practical book. It had a ton of questions that we wouldn't think of normally. Some were about the small things like pet peeves. It makes a big difference when you talk about these ahead of time!

Another thing that you can do is talk to people. I'm talking about even more than the people you ask to do your marriage counseling. If they're married, they have opinions and insights into marriage. Learn from those who have gone before you. If you know older couples, they have years of experience to share. If you have friends who got married recently, they are great to discuss the beginning of marriage with because they'll help you understand more about the coming changes. Plus, it will build connections. People want to share their experiences, so all you have to do is ask.

The important thing is to invest a lot into your future marriage. Most couples put the majority of their time into preparing for the wedding. I don't disagree with this; the wedding is important. I know mine was important. However, when you neglect the mental and spiritual preparation it'll take for the day-to-day highs and lows of marriage, your first year may be tougher than you thought. It won't be as easy as you anticipated to forgive your hot spouse every day.

Do yourself a favor and get yourself ready.

RESOURCES

Here is the article on premarital preparation:

WebMD: www.webmd.com/women/news/20030404/premarital-counseling-builds-better-union#1

36

PREPARING FOR THE BIG DAY

....

When Bailey and I got engaged, it was an exciting time. The anticipation for choosing everything involved with the wedding was fun! I will say though, doing all of the preparation for the wedding while finishing (more like surviving) my last semester of engineering was mentally taxing.

Bailey loved choosing all the big things: colors, bridesmaid dresses, groomsmen attire, flowers, location, look of reception, and endless other details. I basically helped with two things: preparing the ceremony (songs, Bible verses, vows, etc.) and... ok, maybe just one thing. I can't remember, to be honest. Women have the capability of processing a lot of information all at once. I got tired of wedding planning within a month of getting engaged. Every time we met up, it was about planning the wedding. My mental space for the wedding decreased very quickly. I always told myself that the benefit of being a wedding videographer on the side was that I would get to pick and choose the things I liked from all the weddings I had attended. As it turned out, I didn't have a whole lot of opinions, so I left most decisions to Bailey.

I (kind of) tried helping more! But I pretty much stuck to what I was good at. And that was preparing for after the wedding. Here are the things you need to research and do prior to the wedding:

1. Find a place to live
2. Get the marriage license
3. Plan the honeymoon
4. Prepare a combined budget

FIND A PLACE TO LIVE
Assuming you aren't already living together. You can start your marriage where you currently live or where your spouse lives. Bailey

Add Marriage on Top of All This

and I both lived with our parents, so that wouldn't work. We got possession of an apartment about a month before the wedding.

GET THE MARRIAGE LICENSE

In Ohio, we had to get our marriage license within sixty days of the wedding date and within the county in which we were going to get married. It was actually a bigger deal than I thought it would be. We got the paperwork and filled it out, which required us to sign that we weren't within a certain degree of relation to one another. Then we had to raise our right hands and actually swear to it. But it took no more than 30 minutes, and then we had our license. Technically, we could have gone straight to our pastor's house from there and gotten married. We didn't, as tempting as it was. Plus, you know, we sent out a bunch of invites.

To get the license, you are generally required to bring your birth certificate, photo identification (such as your driver's license, state ID or your passport), your Social Security number, and proof of residence (such as a bank statement or a utility bill).

PLAN YOUR HONEYMOON

I know it pretty much goes without saying, but make sure you've got all the details down for your honeymoon. Talk to your fiancé/e and figure out a place and activities that you both will enjoy. Also, ensure you have plenty of relaxation time to get to *know* each other. You don't want to get married and then spend the next week or two tiring yourselves out, trust me. Just ensure that you have the hotels booked and travel plans set (like flights). Also, not only should you have an idea about what the honeymoon will cost, you should also have a plan for how you are going to pay for it. Don't go paying for it with credit cards if you don't have a budget set. Plan in advance what you want to do so that you have the time necessary to save up for it. As said in the budgeting chapter, if you don't have a plan, it's easy to overspend.

PREPARE A COMBINED BUDGET

On the topic of budget, make a mock budget ahead of the wedding so that from day one of being Mr. and Mrs., you both have a plan for your money! Get all the details from your fiancé/e about their monthly income, savings, and debt. Make a plan for how to pay off the debt

Graduated and Clueless

and have a dream meeting about what is important to you when it comes to finances. We didn't necessarily have a dream meeting; however, we did have plenty of discussions over the months leading up to the wedding about how we were going to use our money post-wedding.

The important thing is that you have a plan. I can't stress it enough. It certainly helped us because after coming back from the honeymoon, I knew *exactly* what to do with that first paycheck we both received. If you want more information about developing your budget, go to the budget section of this book. Your budget will prove to be one of the single most important life-hacks you will ever use!

37

THINGS TO CHANGE AFTER MARRIAGE

One of the most confusing parts about getting ready for our wedding was knowing what needed to be changed legally and otherwise to make the transition smooth. There were really three things that we needed to ensure we changed.

1. Bank Accounts
2. Tax information
3. Social Security Administration Information

BANK ACCOUNTS
Bank accounts are vital to combine because you are now a married couple. Biblically speaking, you are "one flesh" after marriage, so everything you do needs to be in view of you as one team. You're married, so your finances need to be married, including your bank accounts.

"But it's ok. We can handle paying for things with two separate accounts." Don't use this excuse because, though it may be true, it opens up a lot of possible problems. I have a friend who has been married for five years now and they still have separate accounts. And I know for a fact that he doesn't know where the majority of his wife's paycheck goes every month. When you have accounts together, it boosts your trust and keeps you accountable to one another. It's not his money and her money. Now, it's our money and it needs to be treated as such!

TAX INFORMATION
The next thing you're going to want to do post-marriage is change your tax information. Go to your employer and request a new W-4 form from your HR department. Change your marital status. Granted, you can leave your information the same, but the benefit of updating

Graduated and Clueless

your status with the IRS is that it will decrease the amount of money that your employer automatically withholds for taxes. Speaking from experience, getting our withholdings down to the minimum is vital because it leaves more to go to retirement funds, home savings, tuition for Bailey and drones for me.

SOCIAL SECURITY ADMINISTRATION INFORMATION
The last major thing you need to do is update your information with the social security administration *if* you are a woman and *if* you plan to change your last name to the last name of your husband. The sooner you do this, the easier it will be for doing things like combining bank accounts and taking care of taxes.

RESOURCES
Check this out for changing your Social Security information:
www.faq.ssa.gov/en-US/Topic/article/KA-01981

38

WHAT DOES MY TIME LOOK LIKE AFTER THE WEDDING?

We got married in the summer. It was an ideal time because Bailey wasn't in school and we got to spend almost every evening and weekend together for our first couple of months as husband and wife. It was a great way of understanding what being married was really like.

As we moved into our third month of marriage, I started to realize something: I needed more "me time." I've found that it's a very important time that helps keep me from burning out. If you get married, it will probably seem selfish for you to need more time to yourself. But in reality, time alone helps you keep your "sanity" for lack of a better term (I don't want Bailey to think she drives me crazy if she reads this). Having time to yourself will actually make you a better spouse. Marriage is a give and take. Sure, it's sacrificial (sometimes REALLY sacrificial), but if all you're doing is giving your time and your energy to your spouse, I guarantee you will need a way to recharge, especially if you are an introvert. This is where personality types kick in. Let me break it down for the introverts and the extroverts.

Introverts: I've already said what I need to say to you. I'm an introvert, so I know what it's like; we need some time by ourselves; otherwise, we may go crazy! Now, fortunately, this isn't difficult for Bailey and me. We are both introverts, so if one needs some time alone, the other is (mostly) more than happy to grant that time. We both benefit!

Extroverts: You're a bit trickier. I'm not an extrovert, but I will speak to you about this topic in the best way I can. You all recharge your batteries by spending time with others. However, if you are married to an introvert, a sacrificial part of your relationship (at least for you) will be giving them time to recharge… alone. If you're an extrovert

Graduated and Clueless

married to an extrovert, I have no idea what to say to you. Just go spend tons of time together.

Keep this in mind: people recharge differently, and a sacrificial act for you will depend on your personality type. For those couples that are a mix of introvert and extrovert, you're going to have a bit of extra give and take. Take Steve and Lauren. Steve, who is an extrovert, needs to give time to Lauren, who is an introvert, for her to recharge by herself. But Lauren also needs to give her time to Steve so that he can recharge socially with someone. Balance this time and you'll be on your way to a healthy marriage relationship!

39

WHAT DO OUR ROLES LOOK LIKE?

This can be a touchy subject in today's day and age. Here's the deal, I don't think that roles necessarily have to look exactly like they have for the last six millennia. But this is a big topic and needs to be discussed before marriage! Otherwise, it may cause some conflict unnecessarily.

For Bailey and me, things differ and our gender roles pretty much vary based on what needs done… mostly. I still take out the trash because Bailey doesn't like to. I still shovel the walkway when there's snow. I do most of the dishes. Bailey still makes the meals because I'm just not a cook (though I'm told that's a bad excuse). But we share a lot of other responsibilities. We both do laundry. We both clean the bathroom.

You both need to discuss this in depth prior to marriage because it'll diminish a bit of potential conflict. And if you're married already but haven't discussed it, talk about it today! Here are some questions to ask each other:

1. What are your expectations for what your own role is/will be?
2. What about your expectations for me?
3. What things do neither of us like to do and how can we compromise on those?

40

HOW DO FRIENDSHIPS WORK NOW?

You may be in love and want to spend all your time together, but friendships are incredibly important to maintain after the wedding! If you only spend time with your spouse, you will only grow at the rate your spouse grows. And you will only get their opinions.

Growing with and understanding the opinions of your spouse is important because biblically, you're now yoked together and considered to be one (Mark 10:8-9). I admit that after the wedding, you and your spouse need to spend an enormous amount of time together. The Bible even talks about this in Deuteronomy 24:5 (NIV) where it says, "If a man has recently married, he must not be sent to war or have any other duty laid on him. For one year he is to be free to stay at home and bring happiness to the wife he has married." It's saying that you need to invest a lot of time into your marriage—especially at the beginning—to ensure that it is built on a strong foundation!

However, this doesn't change the importance of keeping the friends you had before marriage. That is, assuming they are friendships that continue to grow and sharpen one another (see Chapter #4 on deep friendships). Personally, I believe it's unhealthy to only spend time with your spouse outside of work. Friendships will help you become a better spouse, assuming that you aren't complaining about your spouse when spending time with friends. In my case, my friends encourage and challenge me to become a better husband.

For Bailey and me, our friendships did drop off a bit after getting married because we did have to spend time with one another (not to mention that we wanted to spend time together). That is a sacrifice that has to be made for marriage and it'll probably help if your friends understand that there will be a drop in the time you spend together directly after the wedding. But don't drop them entirely (intentionally

Add Marriage on Top of All This

or unintentionally) because they will help you through this enormous change!

Bailey and I let each other get together with friends by ourselves. Normally, it'll happen when the other is busy at work or school anyways, but we support each other in pursuing those friendships. You just need to ensure that friendships don't take an unnecessary amount of time away from your spouse.

I was one of the first among my friends to get married, which honestly scared me. Everyone was in the same stage of life up to the point of the wedding. I was afraid the rest of my friends would start feeling like I was not a part of the group anymore—like they couldn't relate to me. How was that going to affect my friendships?

If you're in a similar circumstance, intentionally seek your friends out, especially if they are not married. That's what I've been trying to do since the wedding. When we talk, I try not to be shallow in conversation but to ask deeper questions. I try to show interest in their lives and their problems. And for some of them, I even said, "Hey, I know that I'm married now and that may change the overall feeling of our relationship, but I want you to know that I'm here for you whenever you need me. I might not be able to spend as much 'hang time' with you, but our friendship is valuable to me and I want you to know that." It's important to realize that our relationships really *are* different to an extent. I can't relate to their singleness as much as another single guy can. Sometimes they actually need another single guy with whom to discuss things. But we still get to learn things from each other which is why we are friends!

Keep up the friendships. They will serve you well if you care for them.

41

HOW DOES FAMILY TIME LOOK NOW?

Leading up to the wedding, I knew family time was going to look differently than it had. Not only was my family going to have to share me with Bailey and add her into the ranks of Bales, they would also have to share me with Bailey's family. Time together would be cut significantly, and I wasn't sure how that was going to turn out. I love my family, so this concerned me.

Fortunately, both of our families are incredibly understanding. Neither of them try to hold us on psychological ropes, making us feel bad if we can't make it to a gathering. Our parents understand the struggle we face because they experienced it.

Since the wedding, both families have been incredibly gracious. It hasn't been difficult to deal with anyone at all. We get to see Bailey's family every Sunday at church and my family every Sunday for brunch afterwards. Granted, though we generally see both families every week, we pull back sometimes from joining them for meals or other activities if Bailey and I haven't gotten to relax and spend time with one another recently.

However, like most other categories of this book, intentionality is one of the biggest aspects to managing family time. For instance, my dad and I have breakfast every other week in order to catch up and discuss books we've read and dreams we have for the future. My sister, brother, and I will meet every other Saturday so that we can help one another maintain goals we've set for business and personal growth.

Intentionality has become a must for me in the last year; otherwise I would lose a lot of the strength of relationships I've had. Here's the key: discuss family time with your spouse. Communicate. What expectations do you have? How can you manage your time with both families without one missing out more? Work hard to curb any hurt feelings on either side which could lead to bitterness.

42

HOW DO WE HANDLE HOLIDAYS NOW?

I like tradition and my family likes it, too. We've got a lot of tradition revolving holidays and their respective seasons. My extended family normally gathers for a meal and games. I love that time with my family, but going into marriage, I knew it would likely change. Bailey's extended family actually lives in Iowa, so holidays usually look different for them, normally involving a lot of travel.

What we had to do is have a spouse meeting and discuss together what the important things were to us and to our families. As I said in the last chapter about managing the time with family, our families both have been very gracious with us and knew the holidays might look significantly different than normal. I've lived through a whopping one (1) season of holidays as a married man and I'm not sure I can say much more than this: compromise is the key. You're both going to have to do some give and take (again?) on what you like and find important.

Our own experience involved us sticking around my family's house for Christmas but then traveling out to Iowa to see Bailey's mom's side for New Year's, despite Bailey's family having traveled out to see her dad's side over Christmas. Christmas was bittersweet for Bailey. She got to spend it with her new husband (yay!), but she didn't even get to see her family on Christmas. Similarly, I didn't get to experience anything surrounding New Year's with my family per usual. But we had an excellent time. Memories were made. New memories. Traditions were started (is it actually a tradition if it has only happened one year?). Time was spent with family. Communication (again) is key.

Discuss what's important to you and your spouse surrounding the holidays. Focus on what you can sacrifice for your spouse to make their holiday special. However, find a way to compromise on some things so that both of you can look back on a special holiday season, even with the changes.

43

FIND THE TIME TO TALK DEEPLY

It is easy after the wedding to stop trying nearly as hard to "date" your spouse. I mean, you already sealed the deal, right? Right, but take it from someone with experience—my work to keep dating Bailey after the wedding went down quite a bit. Part of that was due to budgeting constraints, but that shouldn't change our level of pursuit.

You may have budgeting constraints, too. Bailey and I literally have only $30 budgeted per month for restaurants (eating together or separately) and $30 for dates. Not much! As a dating couple, I didn't worry what I was spending on dates. I mean, gotta seal the deal, right? But we now have goals we want to save towards together (house, etc).

Even with budgeting constraints, you can have deep discussions and ask each other questions. Bailey and I like to go on walks. For one, they are super cheap! But on the walks, we get to talk a lot about things that are going on and discuss dreams we have for the future. I was great at this before marriage (worse now, but I still try) when I would ask every Monday if there was anything Bailey had been wanting to talk about or ask me. This was and continues to be an excellent way of talking about things that we might have to push ourselves a bit to bring up. Sometimes it's fun; sometimes it's not. Like something the spouse does that bugs the other.

The point of this chapter is to encourage you to push yourself to continue dating your spouse. It doesn't have to be expensive. You just need to connect on a regular basis. Plan those times strategically. I haven't been great at this recently because I tend to ask Bailey "future dream" questions as we're falling asleep (pun intended). I am notorious for starting to talk, then drifting off rather quickly. Bailey literally told me recently "You know, you can ask me these questions at other times. Your answers are really disjointed and you don't normally finish because you fall asleep first." Whoops.

PART X

NEVER STOP DREAMING

You know what's integral to your enthusiasm in life? Dreaming. Dreaming about what you want to do for a living. Dreaming about who you want to be. Dreaming about the relationships you want to have.

I already used this quote in the jobs and passion section of this book, however it deserves another shoutout. Author and civil rights leader, Howard Thurman said, "Don't ask what the world needs. Ask what makes you come alive, and go do it. Because what the world needs is people who have come alive."

My dreams make me come alive more than anything. Well, maybe anything aside from living out those dreams. When I dream and strive for new goals is when I am especially passionate. When are you most passionate? What dreams keep you alive? Because you need to keep those dreams alive no matter what.

44

WHAT'S NEXT?

Recently, I was telling a friend's mom about the goals I had made at the beginning of the year and how they were going remarkably well (I haven't been great at "New Year's Resolutions" in the past so this is really exciting). She proceeded to congratulate me and say, "That's great! I'm proud of you kids and how you are ambitious to make goals and go after them. At my age, you don't do that much anymore."

I was slightly shocked. She seemed to have lost her dreams. I realize that she may have been in a season of life where she was contented with her work and family. There is a lot to say about contentment! Contentment is critical to your life outlook. Lately, Bailey and I have discussed our gratefulness extensively, and when we go to bed every night, we thank God for the blessings He's given us. We even thank Him for the little things like a warm place to live, the resources to get an education, and a comfortable bed. We are incredibly grateful for where we are in life.

But there is something I want you to understand very clearly. Contentment is powerful and necessary; however, that doesn't mean you can't dream and strive for new goals. That's what I'm doing. And I'm going to continue doing it well into my later years (God willing). This is an area in which I want to encourage you. I want you to *never stop dreaming*. Someone posed this question to me recently: "What goal do you have that is so big that only God can make it happen?" That is a profound question and I continue to struggle with it. I have big goals and big dreams, but I'll be honest, not one of them is unbelievably crazy.

In this day, people are willing to dream, but they aren't willing to jump out and *do* something. After their higher education (or not), they aren't willing to put in the work to learn something new. They think that learning is tough and they'd sometimes prefer a job that has security and doesn't require too much thinking. But what if…

… you loved the job you worked at every day?
… you felt your work was impacting those around you in incredible ways?
… what you did challenged you to learn more and pursue new opportunities?
… at the end of your life, you had no regrets about how you spent it?

These are all things I want for my life. And I'm making it a point to pursue new opportunities, push myself in learning, and *do* things that will bring me to my goals. That requires everyday discipline. It's not easy by any means, but nothing that's worth doing is easy.

A book I once read said that everyone's got potential, but not everyone does something with that potential. In the physical world, there are two kinds of energy: kinetic energy and potential energy. Kinetic energy is the energy of something in motion. Potential energy is the energy that has the potential to put something in motion. Thus, when something begins to move, potential energy is being converted to kinetic energy.

Think about an apple on a tree. It has potential energy because gravity causes it to have the potential to fall. But the key is this: something that has potential energy will only begin to move if something causes it to move. This is due to Isaac Newton's first law: "Objects at rest stay at rest unless acted upon by an outside force. Objects in motion stay in motion unless acted upon by an outside force."

The only way an apple will fall is if its stem weakens and gravity causes it to fall. For a car in motion, the thing that stops it from rolling is friction. You, my friend, have unbelievable potential. The thing is, you have the ability to be the outside force causing movement. And if you begin to move, you'll gain momentum, making it easier to continue moving. But you've got to start.

In his bestselling book titled *Good to Great*, author and researcher Jim Collins discusses the concept of momentum when it comes to a company. He says this:

Graduated and Clueless

> Picture a huge, heavy flywheel—a massive metal disk mounted horizontally on an axle, about 30 feet in diameter, 2 feet thick, and weighing about 5,000 pounds. Now imagine that your task is to get the flywheel rotating on the axle as fast and long as possible.
>
> Pushing with great effort, you get the flywheel to inch forward, moving almost imperceptibly at first. You keep pushing and, after two or three hours of persistent effort, you get the flywheel to complete one entire turn.
>
> You keep pushing, and the flywheel begins to move a bit faster, and with continued great effort, you move it around a second rotation. You keep pushing in a consistent direction. Three turns ... four ... five ... six ... the flywheel builds up speed ... seven ... eight ... you keep pushing ... nine ... ten ... it builds momentum ... eleven ... twelve ... moving faster with each turn ... twenty ... thirty ... fifty ... a hundred.
>
> Then, at some point—breakthrough! The momentum of the thing kicks in your favor, hurling the flywheel forward, turn after turn ... whoosh! ... its own heavy weight working for you. You're pushing no harder than during the first rotation, but the flywheel goes faster and faster. Each turn of the flywheel builds upon work done earlier, compounding your investment of effort. A thousand times faster, then ten thousand, then a hundred thousand. The huge heavy disk flies forward, with almost unstoppable momentum (164-165).

This portrays how unbelievably powerful momentum can be. Once you start moving, momentum keeps you moving without putting as much work in. This isn't to say that it will be easy. As the second part of Newton's first law says, an object will stay in motion unless acted on by an outside force. Unfortunately, there are many things that act on our motion and momentum. Life never ceases to throw challenges at you. Family problems, marital issues, and work challenges are some of life's favorite ways to slow your motion.

It's okay to slow down. Sometimes you have to. But, you must remember that as life's problems slow you down like friction slows down a car, you still have to put energy into keeping your momentum up. This means continuing to learn, invest in people, and connect with

Never Stop Dreaming

God on a regular basis if you're a Christian. One of the biggest ways to continue your momentum is to spend time with the people that will help you stay in motion. As I quoted Jim Rohn in an earlier chapter, "You are the average of the five people you spend the most time with."

If you spend your valuable time with people who will encourage you in your journey and help you stay in motion, you will be putting yourself in an environment that is conducive to momentum. If you spend time with those who say you can't do it and who don't believe in your goals, it'll slow you down.

This book may be finished, but your life, God willing, is far from over. Find what your passion is and pursue it. Seek God's will in your life and look for his guidance. But don't be apathetic. Don't wait to do something. Just *do* it, to borrow the Nike catchphrase. I once heard a wise man say, "It's easier to turn a car around if it's moving." Get your car moving and it'll be easier to get it turned around if it needs to be pointed in a different direction. And don't ever stop dreaming. Please, never stop dreaming.

THANK YOU FOR READING GRADUATED AND CLUELESS!

Will you write a review?

I want to know what you honestly think. All you have to do is go to this book's page on Amazon and give it some stars. That's how people notice. Did you find it informational and helpful? Let people know. Did you think it didn't touch the tough topics graduates are facing? Put that in a review.

These will help me in understanding preferences of information and the overall knowledge gap after graduation. Just please don't attack me or my intentions behind the writings of this book. And don't attack, my grammar! either!

COMMUNICATE WITH ME!

Care to let me know personally what you thought of the book? Email me at graduatedandclueless@gmail.com and I'll send you a response! I have every intention to work on an updated version of this book in the future. If you think of something you believe would be beneficial to other graduates, send me a note. I'll keep it in mind for when I work on an update.

Also, I have a blog in which I write every week about the things we graduates face after college. If you'd like to check it out, I'd love to earn your trust and readership. You can see it at www.CalebBale.com.

CHAPTER NOTES

CHAPTER 2
1. "How to Buy a House." *DaveRamsey.com*. Web. 11 Mar. 2018.
2. "12 Questions to Ask Before Renting an Apartment." *Apartments.com*. CoStar Group, Inc., 11 Jul. 2017. Web. 17 Apr. 2018.
3. Evans, Julie Ryan. "Real Estate Agent Fees: Who Pays the Bill?" *Realtor.com*. National Association of REALTORS, 13 Jun. 2017. Web. 14 Jul. 2018.

CHAPTER 3
1. "How Much Can Buying Generic Brands Save You at the Grocery Story?" *DaveRamsey.com*. Web. 7 Apr. 2018.

CHAPTER 6
1. Clifton, Jim. "The World's Broken Workplace." *Gallup*. 13 Jun. 2017. Web. 16 Apr. 2018.

CHAPTER 7
1. "Exercise and Stress: Get Moving to Manage Stress." *Mayo Clinic*. Mayo Foundation for Medical Education and Research, 8 Mar. 2018. Web. 16 Apr. 2018.

CHAPTER 10
1. Beaudine, Bob. *The Power of Who*. New York: Hachette Book Group, 2009. Print.

CHAPTER 11
1. Godin, Seth. *Linchpin*. New York: Penguin Group, 2010. Print.

CHAPTER 12
1. "Vehicle Coverages." *DVM.org*. Web. 21 Apr. 2018.
2. "How Much Car Insurance Do You Really Need?" *DaveRamsey.com*. Web. 14 Apr. 2018.

Notes

CHAPTER 13
1. "Coverage for pre-existing conditions." *HealthCare.gov*. Web. 21 Jun. 2018.

CHAPTER 15
1. "Term Life Vs. Whole Life Insurance." *DaveRamsey.com*. Web. 21 Apr. 2018.
2. Hogan, Chris. *Retire Inspired*. Brentwood: Ramsey Press, 2016. Print.

CHAPTER 18
1. Glenn, Alex. "Understanding Homeowner's Insurance." *NerdWallet*. 25 Mar. 2016. Web. 2 May 2018.

CHAPTER 19
1. "Identity Theft Protection Services." *Federal Trade Commission*. Mar. 2018. Web. 14 Apr. 2018.

CHAPTER 20
1. Lerner, Michele. "How to Choose an Insurance Deductible." *Bankrate*. 17 Dec. 2012. Web. 25 Apr. 2018.

CHAPTER 21
1. George, Eddie. "Even the Pros Need a Plan (Special Guest Eddie George)." *ChrisHogan360.com*. Ramsey Solutions, 13 Sept. 2017. Web. 14 Jul. 2018.
2. Miller, Donald. *Building a Storybrand*. New York: HarperCollins Publishers, 2017. Print.

CHAPTER 23
1. Ramsey, Dave. *The Total Money Makeover*. Nashville: Thomas Nelson, 2003. Print.
2. "Average Credit Score in America: 2018 Report." *ValuePenguin*. Web. 14 Apr. 2018.
3. "Average Auto Loan Interest Rates: 2018 Facts & Figures." *ValuePenguin*. Web. 14 Apr. 2018.

Notes

CHAPTER 26
1. Alcorn, Randy. *The Treasure Principle.* Colorado Springs: Multnomah Books, 2001. Print.
2. University of Zurich. "Generous people live happier lives." *ScienceDaily.com.* ScienceDaily, 11 Jul. 2017. Web. 20 Jul. 2018.

CHAPTER 34
1. Wolfinger, Nicholas H. "Counterintuitive Trends in the Link Between Premarital Sex and Marital Stability." *IFStudies.org.* 6 Jun. 2016. Web. 15 Apr. 2018.
2. Stanton, Glenn. "Premarital Sex and Greater Risk of Divorce." *Focus on the Family.* 2011. Web. 15 Apr. 2018.

CHAPTER 35
1. "Premarital Counseling Builds Better Union." *WebMD.* 4 Apr. 2003. Web. 15 Apr. 2018.

CHAPTER 37
1. "How do I change or correct my name on my Social Security number card?" *Social Security Administration.* 14 Jun. 2018. Web. 15 Apr. 2018.

CHAPTER 44
1. Collins, Jim. *Good to Great.* New York: HarperCollins Publishers, 2001. Print.

Printed in Great Britain
by Amazon

82653990R00078